P9-CFK-021

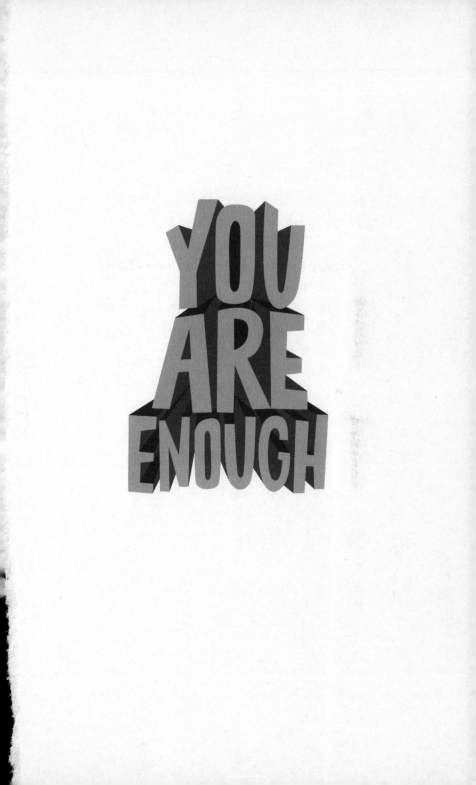

Novels by Jen Petro-Roy

P.S. I Miss You

Good Enough

# YOU ARE ENOUGH

## JEN PETRO-ROY

Feiwel and Friends

New York

The information in this book is not intended to replace the advice of the reader's own physician or other medical professional. You should consult a medical professional in matters relating to health, especially if you have existing medical conditions, and before starting, stopping, or changing the dose of any medication you are taking. Individual readers are solely responsible for their own health care decisions. The author and the publisher do not accept responsibility for any adverse effects individuals may claim to experience, whether directly or indirectly, from the information contained in this book.

The fact that an organization or website is mentioned in the book as a potential source of information does not mean that the author or the publisher endorse any of the information they may provide or recommendations they may make.

A FEIWEL AND FRIENDS BOOK
An imprint of Macmillan Publishing Group, LLC
175 Fifth Avenue, New York, NY 10010

YOU ARE ENOUGH. Copyright © 2019 by Jen Petro-Roy. All rights reserved. Printed in the United States of America by LSC Communications, Harrisonburg, Virginia.

Our books may be purchased in bulk for promotional, educational, or business use. Please contact your local bookseller or the Macmillan Corporate and Premium Sales Department at (800) 221-7945 ext. 5442 or by email at MacmillanSpecialMarkets@macmillan.com.

Library of Congress Cataloging-in-Publication Data
Names: Petro-Roy, Jen, author.
Title: You are enough / Jen Petro-Roy.
Description: New York, NY : Feiwel and Friends, [2019] | Audience: 9–12. | Includes bibliographical references.
Identifiers: LCCN 2018019396 | ISBN 9781250151025 (hardcover)
Subjects: LCSH: Eating disorders in adolescence—Psychological aspects—Juvenile literature. | Eating disorders in adolescence—Treatment—Juvenile literature. | Body image in adolescence—Juvenile literature.
Classification: LCC RC552.E18 P47 2019 | DDC 616.85/2600835—dc23
LC record available at https://lccn.loc.gov/2018019396

Book design by Rebecca Syracuse

Feiwel and Friends logo designed by Filomena Tuosto

First edition, 2019

1 3 5 7 9 10 8 6 4 2

mackids.com

RO456421355

To Ellie and Lucy.
You are everything. I love you.

# TABLE OF CONTENTS

# PART THREE: SOCIETY, ROLE MODELS, FAMILY, AND MEDIA

# HOW TO USE THIS BOOK

**IN THE INTRODUCTION** to this book, I discuss a bit about my own struggles with an eating disorder, and my journey to body acceptance. As you read, please keep in mind that I am writing about my experience alone, about my thoughts and my body alone. In a similar situation, others may have reacted in a different way. The way I related to food and dealt with an eating disorder is no more or less valid than anyone else's.

I am not a medical professional. I do not have experience with every single way food and self-esteem can affect someone's life. The introduction will touch upon my limitations and the ways I worked to fill in the gaps to make this book as helpful to as many different people and populations as possible.

Part One of this book will discuss eating disorders them-selves. What are eating disorders? Who gets them? What other factors can be involved that might make recovery harder? How are eating disorders different from what the media often shows us?

Part Two of this book will discuss different skills and pieces of information that were crucial to *my* recovery, pieces that I hope you can apply to your life through the exercises included at the end of many chapters.

Part Three will cover common situations that you may face while struggling to recover, especially when it comes to people and situations that can seem out of your control (society, friends, family, the media), and will discuss how to combat the bad body image that may accompany your steps forward.

Part Four will talk about what needs to change (both in you and in your environment) as you recover—what steps you may need to take and what boundaries you may need to set up to best guard the way you are learning to feel about your one unique and wonderful self.

The back of the book contains additional resources and source notes, information on scholarship funds for treatment, and recommended books and websites. You can look at this as you are reading or after; it's up to you!

The chapters and subject headings are set up to allow you to skip around the book. If you think a segment in Part

Three will really help you with the place you're in, you can read that section first, without taking away from the message of the rest of the book.

As you read, remember that some people get their eating disorders recognized early while others are never identified. Some families can afford hospital stays and residential treatment, while others struggle with the costs of therapy.

People struggling with eating disorders can be any weight. (I don't like to use the term "normal weight," because what even *is* normal?)

Many people think they don't deserve or need treatment, and some "eating issues" are labeled "not severe enough" for treatment.

Every experience is different, just as every personality and every body is different. The common thread, though, is that we all deserve recovery. No matter your height or weight or body shape or size, no matter what behaviors or thoughts you struggle with, you deserve to recover. You deserve to accept yourself and like yourself and (yes!) even love yourself.

This book is for you. I want it to help you. That's because *you* are important. *You* deserve to read this message and apply these lessons to *your* life.

Let's get started.

# A NOTE ABOUT LANGUAGE

**FIRST OF ALL**, I want to emphasize that language, including terms used to describe specific populations, is always changing. Words that were once seen as insults are now embraced and new words are always being added. For many groups, certain terms can be contentious, embraced by some and rejected by others. Throughout this book, I did the best I could to use terms that would be as clear and welcoming as possible. However, it is possible that some people will have a problem with words I use in this book, and two in particular:

# 1. QUEER

*Queer* is a term with a long and complicated history: It's been used as a slur, but it's also been used in an academic sense and as an identity. Some lesbian, gay, bisexual, transgender, intersex, asexual, aromantic, or pansexual (LGBTQIAP) people also identify as queer, and some don't. Some people feel comfortable using queer as an umbrella term, some prefer an acronym like LGBTQIAP+ or something else.

After listening to a number of people who identify as queer and/or LGBTQIAP+, I've decided to use queer as an umbrella term for a group of people including those who identify as lesbian, gay, bisexual, transgender, nonbinary, questioning, asexual, aromantic, and pansexual.

# 2. FAT

*Fat* is another complicated word. Many people see *fat* as an insult and a cruel thing to call someone. However, like *queer*, *fat* has been reclaimed by fat acceptance activists who embrace the word *fat* and encourage others to use it in a descriptive, positive, or neutral way. Many people prefer it to terms like *overweight* or *obese*, but not everyone does. While some people find the word *fat* empowering, many others still find it hurtful.

That being said, after listening to fat activists, I believe that using the term *fat* rather than *overweight* or *obese* is the most respectful thing to do. So when you see *fat* used throughout the book, know that I am using it as a descriptive term, not as a negative term, nor as a way to insult any group of people.

Also, please note that my use of *queer* and *fat* doesn't mean that all the people interviewed in this book would agree with my usage of the terms.

# INTRODUCTION
## My Journey

### How it started

**THERE WAS A VOICE** in my head for twelve years. More than that, actually. It told me what I should eat and how long I should exercise. It told me that sleep made me lazy and that my body was a work of art I needed to perfect.

It told me that I *was* my body, that everything else about me—my interests, my family, my friends, and my health—didn't matter. All I had to do was be skinny and the world would fall into place.

*It will be easy*, the voice said. *It will be the best thing you'll ever do.*

There wasn't a *real* voice in my head, but it felt that way sometimes. My anxiety when I didn't listen to that voice felt real, too. The anxiety took over my body, making my stomach cramp and my head whirl and my body tense up. Every cell in my brain was devoted to worrying about my body and what I looked like.

I hated it. I loved it.

My eating disorder wasn't my first experience with anxiety or obsession. I had always been a high-strung child. I had friends and had fun and got dirty, but part of me was always worried about *something*:

How my socks didn't feel just right on my feet.

How someone I loved was going to die because I hadn't said "I love you" enough times before bed.

How my friends were just *pretending* to like me.

In sixth grade, a friend and I always joked that if we failed a quiz, it would mean we wouldn't know enough for the big test. If we failed that test, we wouldn't pass the grade. Then we wouldn't go on to high school or college, and we'd end up complete failures.

It was probably a joke to my friend, but it was reality to me. In my mind, every situation was a potential catastrophe. Every person could hurt me.

It wasn't a surprise when I was diagnosed with obsessive-compulsive disorder in the seventh grade. The repeated rituals and fear of cleaning products were pretty obvious signs. My parents hustled me into therapy, and I went on medication to help with my anxiety. After a while, a lot of my behaviors slowed down. My thoughts cleared enough so I could function better.

Back then, I wasn't very worried about my body. I thought about what clothes and shoes I should buy to fit in with my classmates (I thought about that a lot), but I didn't care much about the size I was wearing.

That would come later.

First came the realization that I was still anxious, when I started to prepare for high school and my friends staged an intervention because I was acting too "weird" for them.

I thought they were being mean. They were, of course, but what they didn't realize—what even I didn't yet realize—was that my "weirdness" was a manifestation of my anxiety. I was so afraid my friends didn't really like me that I was sabotaging every interaction we had, acting paranoid and trying too hard to be perfect.

My body issues would come in high school, when I joined the swim team and gained muscles, when my body went through the natural changes of adolescence, and when I broke down in sobs before the school Halloween dance. My friends and I had all dressed up as devils, and I was sure I was the fattest one. I was sure that fat was awful.

My eating disorder would come after I went to college, when I scrutinized my roommates the same way I did my hometown friends, searching for signs that they accepted me. I was so afraid I was boring and unlikable that I retreated into a world of food, weight, and exercise obsession. I thought that could help me avoid any potential rejection.

That's when the feelings of isolation took over and the disease began.

It all started in middle school, though:

My perfectionism.

My fear of not belonging.

My awareness of how I looked.

The anxiety that was always hovering in the background.

I wish I had caught it then. I wish I had reached out for help and admitted what was going on. I wish I knew that my body was not my enemy and that gaining weight isn't a bad thing.

That's what this book is for.

Whether you occasionally worry about your body or you're in the depths of an eating disorder.

Whether you think you might have some eating issues or you absolutely 100 percent know your life needs to change.

There's help out there for you, and there are lots of people who can help you. Taking that first step and talking to a guardian, school counselor, or therapist about how you feel can seem so difficult, but help and support *are* out there.

No matter where you are on your recovery journey, this book is for you. Because you deserve recovery. You deserve a life free from body worries and obsessions and compulsions and anxiety. You don't need an eating disorder.

You are enough just the way you are.

# The journey, the fight

I spent one Christmas in the hospital. While the rest of my family was celebrating together, eating eagerly anticipated holiday treats, I was on the hospital ward, eating according to my meal plan and writing in my journal.

I wasn't supposed to be at the hospital. At that point, I had already been an inpatient for a few weeks, which meant that I was allowed a pass home for Christmas Eve and Christmas Day. I could sleep in my own bed instead of on the limp hospital mattress. I wouldn't have to follow the schedule that was the same every day: Get weighed, shower, eat. Therapy, support group, eat. Support group, nutrition appointment, eat. Eat, eat, and eat some more.

I was supposed to be excited to wake up in my bed on Christmas morning. I was supposed to be excited to open presents with my family and stare at the twinkling lights and talk about whatever "normal" people talk about in the presence of such overwhelming food.

I was not excited.

With every minute at home my anxiety rose, even though I was supposed to be getting "better." I had gained weight at the hospital. I had been eating the suggested meal plan for patients with anorexia for my entire stay, so these twenty-four hours at home were supposed to be easy. If I were a comedian, I'd make a food joke about everything being a piece of cake.

I was supposed to slide back into normalcy as an Olympic diver enters the water, with barely a splash or a ripple. I was supposed to be better now. If not all the way, then enough to enjoy Christmas the way everyone else was. I wasn't supposed to freak out at the amount my mother wanted me to eat. I wasn't supposed to be clenching my fists with anxiety the entire time.

*Supposed to.* Like *should*, it is a phrase that has tortured me for years. We all hear these words in some way. We all think them.

Here are some things I thought:

- Women are supposed to be thin, beautiful, and successful.
- Girls should behave and look nice, be confident but not *too* confident.
- Men are supposed to be muscular and toned.
- Boys should be athletic and popular and successful.

People are expected to fit neatly into categories, and these categories are often binary, with only two options, like woman or man. Girl or boy.

The world often forgets that people are all different. That people naturally come in all shapes and sizes. That boys get eating disorders, too. That gender isn't always binary. That trans people get eating disorders. That queer people get eating disorders. That fat people get eating disorders.

Anyone can have an eating disorder.

When I was younger, I definitely heard *should*s that pertained to me. I focused on the *supposed to* and forgot who I really was. When I got that Christmas pass from the hospital, I forgot where I was on my journey.

At that point in my life, I wasn't ready to do the whole recovery thing on my own. I was too raw. It was all too new. So even though I was *supposed to* be calm, I was totally freaking out.

So I asked my parents to drive me back to the hospital early. Instead of celebrating my favorite holiday, I went back to the eating disorders unit. The hospital was forty minutes away, and it was snowing heavily, but my parents drove me anyway. Because at that point, faced with the idea of spending all day around the indulgences associated with Christmas, I panicked. I retreated. I hid. Just as I had been hiding during my entire illness. I thought then that hiding was a weakness, but I know now that I just needed some extra help. I needed more time.

There was no Christmas tree on the eating disorders unit, only some lights strung along the windows. My family wasn't there, but other patients were, the ones too sick or too new to the program to go home for the holiday. We drew pictures and watched Christmas movies. We ate. We passed the time however we could.

Looking back now, the scene feels lonely. Back then, though, I was relieved. I was happy to spend the holiday season away from my family. I was ecstatic to escape the pressure of having to make choices about food. I wasn't ready to do that on my own yet.

It took me a long time to be fully ready to take care of myself, to truly realize, deep down, that I was worth nurturing and loving and accepting. It took two years in the hospital, off and on, in both partial and full hospitalization programs. It took two stays in residential treatment, each for three months, a year apart. It took medication and visits to therapists and nutritionists. It took relapses and almost ten years of *thinking* I was recovered but still having a lot more work to do.

I'm a work in progress. A messy work in progress that I've started over a thousand times. I've erased things and gone back to earlier sketches. I've stared at my painting so hard that the colors blurred before my eyes. I've been afraid to finish because it might not be perfect. Because there might be mistakes.

There *were* mistakes. I still make mistakes. But I kept going. I keep going. Because the life that I have right now—the worst day that I have right now—is so much more amazing than anything that came before.

As I mentioned, my disordered thoughts transformed into an eating disorder when I went away to college. College was a big change for me. I am *not* a big fan of change. I like to know what to expect. I like planning for things. And when things are good, I want them to stay that way.

I loved high school. I was good at school, and I loved being on the swim team. I fit in. Well, I *thought* I fit in. In reality, I fit in because I worked really, really hard at fitting in. Even with my friends, I was constantly aware of what I said and did.

Was I acting cool enough? Did I sound foolish? Was my shirt in style? Did my body look different from everyone else's?

I shouldn't have had to work that hard to feel good about myself, but it was all I'd ever known. I knew that when I excelled academically and was nice and perky and in a good mood, people liked me. So I always had to be in a good mood. I always had to be "on."

I decided to do the same thing in college. But I worried about what would happen if I presented my "best" self and these new people *still* didn't like me.

What then? My biggest fear was that I'd be rejected, that the gut-level, deep-down fears I had about myself (I was worthless, I was wrong, I wasn't as good as everyone else) would be proven true.

I knew they were true.

They had to be true.

Upon meeting my two roommates, I automatically compared my body with theirs and noticed that they were skinnier. I determined that this made them better and that I'd been right. I wasn't going to fit in.

So I decided to take things one step further. If I lost a little weight, everything would be okay. If I was skinnier, I'd be worthy. I started exercising. I started eating "better." My first morning at college, I woke up early and went to the gym across campus. Two girls in the dorm next door saw me leaving and invited me to go running with them.

*Wow!* I should have thought. *Friends! Just what I want!*

My mind didn't think that, though. My mind was so focused on losing weight to *get* friends that it rejected the fact that potential friends were standing right in front of me. Instead, my mind compelled me to say no and go to the gym instead.

*They won't run long enough for me*, I thought. *I need a better workout if I'm going to lose enough weight to fit in.*

I didn't become friends with those girls. I kept going to the gym. I ran instead of hanging out and watching TV. I ran instead of creating the bonding moments that cement friendships. I left classes early to work out and only ate what I thought I should. I had rules, and I followed them.

You might have rules, too. You might only eat certain foods at certain times. You might diet for a few days and then give up. You might binge on certain days of the week. You might have to wake up early to exercise for a certain number of minutes or do a certain number of crunches, even if your body is screaming for rest. You might know how hard it is to break these rules.

I couldn't break my rules. Not even when I realized I was miserable at school because I hadn't opened myself up enough to let myself fit in. Not when I transferred schools the next year and found that my eating disorder (because that's what it was, even though I hadn't realized or admitted it yet) had followed me. Not when I took a leave of absence from school to enter treatment once my parents found out what was going on.

I thought I'd been so careful. I thought I was hiding what I was doing. I thought everyone believed my lies. I said that I was eating healthier, that I just wanted to lose a little weight. I thought they didn't notice.

They noticed. My family noticed and my friends noticed. They saw me lying and saw me pulling away, saw me canceling plans because I was afraid food would be there.

I was afraid food would be *everywhere*. I was afraid that if I went to a party or opened up about how much I was struggling, how hungry I was and how I couldn't stop myself from restricting food and exercising, someone would take my eating disorder away from me.

The funny thing was that I actually *wanted* my eating disorder gone. I so wanted it gone. I was tired of pushing my body to its limit. I was tired of not sleeping because my bones hurt. I was tired of being hungry. I was tired of always thinking. Always measuring and counting and weighing.

I was tired of never feeling that I was good enough,

never feeling that I was getting closer to a finish line forever out of reach. I never lost enough weight. I never looked as good as I wanted to, as good as my friends and everyone on TV did.

I wanted to be happy.

But I couldn't stop.

One afternoon, I came home from my summer job. I was working at a law firm, answering the phone and typing memos and filing boring papers. I sat all day. I felt like a blob, so I needed—*needed*—to spend my lunch break exercising. I quickly changed into workout clothes, then hopped onto the bike in our basement. I'd have enough time to get in a mini workout before I had to go back, I promised myself. It would hold me over and hold back the anxiety until later.

And it did hold back the anxiety—until my father walked in twenty minutes later. I *never* stopped in the middle of a workout, but I stopped then. I stopped pedaling, sweat dripping down my face. I was busted.

I went into treatment after that. My parents made me go, but deep down I was glad. I was relieved. I knew I was sick. I hated my life the way it was. I hated it, but I couldn't stop myself from self-destructing. Not on my own.

Sometimes it felt as if I would die of anxiety if I didn't skip a meal, even though I knew I was getting sicker and sicker by the day. I needed to escape. I wanted to escape. I wanted to be free, like my friends were. The ones who could eat junk food at a sleepover. The ones who could skip a workout if they were tired and wouldn't freak out if they didn't know what restaurant people were going to more than a day in advance.

When I entered treatment, I was scared and relieved. Scared that the doctors would take away my eating disorder—the one thing that made me feel special—and relieved that they were going to make me eat. Make me rest. I wouldn't have to fight myself anymore.

I thought I was going to walk in the door and be cured.

I thought wrong.


## The path to the other side

Treatment isn't a cure-all. This book won't be a cure-all, either, even though I wish it could be. Treatment *does* help, though. For me, treatment took the form of hospital-ization, and it started me on my journey to recovery. It forced me to admit that I had a problem and gave me the coping mechanisms to use in situations that triggered my anxieties and obsession with my body. I learned methods to calm myself down and worked to unravel why I felt that I wasn't good enough for the world.

I learned about the messages my eating disorder sent me and how to distinguish them from my healthy voice. I went to groups on nutrition and body image, where we made sample meal plans and analyzed advertisements in magazines. I practiced speaking up to my family when they put too much pressure on me and telling my friends what I needed them to do to help my recovery.

I made lists of my goals and dreams, ones that I couldn't accomplish with an eating disorder. I started to remember what was good about me outside of my body.

And I ate. I ate regularly and fed my body so that it could trust me again. I fed my brain so that it started functioning properly. And as I ate, I saw that food didn't kill me. I saw that I didn't gain seven million pounds after eating one meal. That I could wear a different pants size and my friends would still like me. That even if the world told me I had to be a specific size, being—or trying to be—that size was killing me.

And if it didn't kill me, it would kill my spirit. It would kill what makes life worth living.

I learned all this—and then I left the hospital and relapsed.

Things came up in the outside world, situations that made me want to dive back into my eating disorder:

- Someone commented on my weight gain.
- A friend went on a diet.
- My parents kept staring at me while I ate.
- I wasn't invited to a party and felt left out.

I relapsed, and I wasn't able to pull myself out of the hole by myself. I got stuck again, so stuck that I needed more treatment. There are lots of types of treatment, but the right step for me was to go back to the hospital.

After I was discharged, I relapsed again. I repeated this cycle for a while, through various forms of treatment. Some people go through a similar process. Some people don't go to treatment but work toward recovery on their own instead. Some people relapse, while some recover on the "first try."

While the recovery process may vary, one truth is generally the same for everyone: It's hard to leave an eating disorder behind. It's hard to accept your body. So even though our experiences may differ, you may understand what I went through.

I left residential treatment the second time humbled. I had hit my rock bottom. I wanted a life. I wanted to go back to school. I wanted to be with my friends, who were having adventures without me. *They* had experiences and memories. *They* were living their lives.

My memories were of treatment and meal plans and body image homework. I wanted more. I wanted life, regardless of the weight I had to be in order to live it. I wanted myself back.

That's when things started changing.

There was still a part of me that wanted to be skinny.

There was still a part of me that felt like I wasn't enough. But I ignored those parts. I focused on what I wanted and what I needed to do to get there. I had goals and dreams. I wanted to get married and have kids. I wanted to be a writer. I wanted to go out with friends and laugh and swim and run without worrying about how many calories I was burning.

I wanted to eat my favorite foods. I wanted to sleep in without feeling like a sloth. (Sleep is good. My body likes sleep.) I wanted real life more than I wanted the fake life I was living in the fake body I had created.

I left residential treatment and followed my meal plan. I was honest about the times I didn't follow it, so I could get back on track. I gained weight. I freaked out about gaining weight. I freaked out for a long, long time.

But eventually I realized that I actually felt better when I wasn't so skinny. I had more energy. My sense of humor was back, and I laughed more. I wasn't cold all the time, and clothes fit me better. And as I ate and gained, I felt less anxious. Things leveled off. My weight stabilized.

It was a miracle! (Okay, not really. But to me, it felt like one.)

That wasn't the end of my recovery journey, though, because after a few years, I realized that I had more work to do. I had started internalizing society's messages again, started feeling like I wasn't good enough. I was exercising a bit more than I should and my eating became disordered. I wasn't doing anything awful or "sick," but I was on a quasi diet, not eating what I was really hungry for. I was trying to control myself, working hard to keep my body at the size that *I* wanted it to be, rather than the size that *it* wanted to be.

Bodies know these things. They have set points, where they're biologically supposed to be for maximum health and comfort.[1] Bodies are like machines. Not quite robot level, but pretty cool anyway. When you restrict your food, you feel hungry. Your metabolism slows down so your body can hold on to the calories you've already consumed. On the other hand, when you eat a lot, you might not feel hungry later.

Our bodies are amazing. And I needed to trust mine.

So I adjusted my actions and my mind again. I eased up on the exercise. I listened to my body. I let myself eat more because my body wanted more. I let my body find itself.

I let *me* find myself. I thought I was recovered, but I wasn't. Not all the way. I still had work to do. Sometimes, even now, I realize that I still have work to do. I'm human, and I exist in this very complicated world. I change. I adjust. I adapt.

I grow.

I'm not perfect. But I am recovered. For me, recovery

doesn't mean that I never get stressed out. Everyone gets stressed out; that's part of being human. But now, when I'm anxious, I know there are so many things out there that will calm me down more than restricting food or obsessing ever could.

When I compare myself with someone else, I try to identify what it is that I'm jealous of, then figure out how to fulfill that need in a way that doesn't make me feel awful. If I'm jealous that someone is prettier than I am, I don't necessarily yell at myself. I ask myself what "pretty" means. Do I want a new haircut? Do I need more sleep? Do I need to think about ways that I'm awesome, too?

Because I'm awesome. It took me a long time to realize that, but I finally do. My body is bigger now, and that's not a bad thing. Weight gain isn't bad. I am so much more than the wrapping paper around my heart, and so are you. We are a collection of talents and skills and pluck and drive and kindness. We can overcome obstacles and enjoy life.

When I was in treatment and expressing doubts about recovery, the counselors always told us about the importance of trust:

Trust in recovery and trust in my hunger.

Trust in what my body needs to function and thrive.

Trust that my coping skills work.

Trust that I'm a great person.

They told us to give recovery a try. To go all in. "If you eventually recover and don't like it, then you can always go back," they said. "You can go back to obsessing about your body. You can hide away from the world for the rest of your life. Just give recovery a try first. I promise you, you won't want to go back. Once you recover, you'll see. You'll never want to go back."

They were right. I never want to go back. Never.

You won't, either.

Recovery isn't magical. I still have bad body image days. I still feel guilty about not being good enough—not being a good enough writer, mother, friend, *whatever*. I still have hard moments in life—financial stressors and family stressors and so much more. But I *live*, regardless of these feelings and situations. I live and eat and move and make memories. I used the lessons that I learned in treatment until I internalized them. Until those beliefs of worthiness and enoughness became part of me.

You deserve to learn those lessons, too, whether you've been in treatment or are soon going to treatment or can't afford treatment. Whether you have slightly disordered eating or a diagnosable eating disorder. Whether you binge or purge or starve or overexercise. You deserve to know that whatever you've done, however you feel, you don't have to feel like that anymore.

In this book, you won't find any information about what

my lowest weight was or how many calories I ate. I don't talk about how long I exercised or what sizes I wore.

Those numbers don't matter. They don't matter because they didn't define me then and they don't define me now. But they also don't matter because you can be sick regardless of your weight. You can have a disordered relationship with food no matter how often you do certain actions. I don't want you to compare yourself with me or anyone else. I want you to focus on what's healthy for *you* and what is or isn't working in *your* life.

That's what matters. You matter.

This book won't cure you. No book can do that. You are the only one who can help yourself. And that's the amazing thing: You can help yourself. You can! You don't have to be thin to love yourself. You don't have to look or be a certain way. You can stop hurting yourself and hating yourself regardless of your size or your weight.

You can live regardless of your size or your weight.

You *are* enough.

## My limitations

You may never be fixed. I may never be fixed.

Everyone in this world has something to work on, though. We all have things we can be better at. That doesn't mean we're broken. It doesn't mean we're hopeless cases.

It means that we're human, just like everybody else. I am not a perfect person, and I most likely did not write a perfect book.

I am writing this book as a straight, white female. I come from an upper-middle class background. I am cis, meaning that my gender matches the gender I was assigned at birth. I am married. I suffered from anorexia and excessive exercise.

I am privileged in many ways, and I did not and do not experience many of the things that readers of this book may experience. I am different from you. You are different from other readers, too.

In this book, I am not talking only to people with experiences like mine. This book is for *everyone* who suffers from disordered eating. This book is for all people who worry about their body and think that they are not enough.

Because of my limited background, I made it a point to research other experiences. I have talked to doctors, counselors, and nutritionists who work with various populations and varied eating disorders. I have talked with advocacy workers in the queer community.

I have interviewed people of color and men with eating disorders. I have spoken with transgender men and women, with people of varying sexual orientations, and with genderqueer individuals about their struggles with body image. I have spoken with individuals in the fat acceptance and Health at Every Size movements to discuss the importance of accepting your body size as it is and as it's meant to be.

It is my hope that regardless of your experience, you will be able to see your struggles mirrored in this book. You may not be able to relate to every chapter, and you may not identify with every piece of advice. But no matter who you are and which pieces of this book you relate to, your struggle matters. You are not alone.

That's the funny thing about eating disorders: When you're in the middle of your struggle, you think that you're the only person in the world who could ever feel this way. And, yes, portions of your experience *are* unique. You're the only one who has walked your path. But your emotions and fears are also universal. Lots of people think they don't matter. Lots of people don't feel at home in their bodies, whether they're unhappy with their weight or are dealing with a chronic illness.

Individual circumstances can make recovery more challenging, especially when eating disorders are misunderstood or overlooked.

Research into eating disorders in the queer population is still limited. However, the National Eating Disorders Association reports that as early as age twelve, "gay, lesbian, and bisexual teens may be at higher risk of binge-eating and purging than heterosexual peers."[2] Compared with other populations, gay men report more disordered eating behaviors such as laxative use, fasting, and purging.

Transgender people report more disordered eating than cis people, and they have to deal with more than one type of body image issue: both size and the conflict between their assigned gender and the gender they actually are. A 2015 study showed that 16 percent of transgender participants had been diagnosed with an eating disorder.[3] Yet this information is rarely heard in the mainstream.

The eating disorder stereotype is usually a skinny white girl "who wants to be pretty." But what about the boys who are struggling? What about nonbinary people and other queer people? What about people of color?

Some people develop eating disorders after they are diagnosed with a disease like diabetes, which demands an extreme focus on food.[4]

Fat people can have eating disorders.

Eating disorders do not discriminate based on body size, skin color, socioeconomic background, sexual orientation, health, ability, or gender.

We need to get familiar with the variety of people who have eating disorders so we can recognize symptoms in ourselves and in others. So we can stop making these distinctions and move toward becoming one community working together to erase eating disorders, remove barriers to eating disorder treatment, and get rid of factors that contribute to eating disorders, such as size-based discrimination and the pressure to adhere to societal expectations.

We all suffer, and we all struggle. We all feel out of place. But with that bond comes hope. With that connection comes the knowledge that you don't have to feel like this forever. Others have traveled this road and emerged into the sunlight. Others have healed.

Even if you don't connect to everything in this book, it is my hope that every chapter will add something important to the conversation about body image and self-esteem. That in the end, *you* will find hope and realize that every part of you is enough.

# PART ONE

About Eating Disorders

# CHAPTER 1

## What Are Eating Disorders?

**YOU MIGHT PICK** up this book already knowing a lot about eating disorders. Or you might pick up this book knowing nothing about the specifics, nothing about the official words that doctors might throw at you. All you know is that something is wrong with your relationship with food.

You don't have to know all the lingo to get better, just as you don't have to be labeled a certain way to have a problem.

Eating disorders cover a wide variety of symptoms and arise because of a variety of factors, as I will discuss later. At their core, though, eating disorders are a collection of symptoms that interfere with your quality of life. If you have an eating disorder, you may worry about your body or about gaining weight or muscle. You may compare yourself to others. When you have anxiety or feel upset, you may find comfort in food—either by restricting it, purging it, or binge-ing on it. These behaviors (along with others) may soothe something inside of you that is hurting.

Some people with eating disorders don't eat enough and become malnourished and sick. Some people with eat-ing disorders eat too much, too quickly, and feel sick. Others eat and then throw up their food, and others are bothered by the textures of certain foods and are unable to eat them. Many people with eating disorders have complex rules about what foods are "safe" to eat and what foods are off-limits. Others might force themselves to exercise past the point of safety.

The criteria for diagnosis are complicated, but if you're able to go to a medical professional, you can be assessed and possibly given a diagnosis. But if you think something might be wrong with the way you eat or exercise, if you think that it may be out of control or disordered in any way, this book is for you. Whether or not you have an official diagno-sis from a doctor, whether or not you believe you're "sick" enough to have an eating disorder, and whether you're thin or fat, if you or someone in your life thinks your eating might be disordered and you think you might have problems with your body image, this book is for you.

When I was sick, I heard many people comment that

they would "love an eating disorder to lose weight." That's not how it works, though. Eating disorders aren't a diet. You can't simply borrow an eating disorder for a while and then return it when you're done. Eating disorders are hard to get rid of. They affect your brain like an addiction, and once you start receiving that sense of comfort from disordered behaviors, it becomes hard to stop these dangerous actions.

You *can* stop, though. If you are reading this book, there is a high chance that you are ready for a change. That you realize that whatever reassurance your eating disorder once provided you isn't worth the discomfort and lack of energy and sadness that now invade your days.

Maybe you're not quite ready to change *yet*, but you recognize that recovery *could* be a possibility someday. (Maybe.) There is nothing wrong with feeling like that. Recovery is a process, and the first step is recognizing that it *can* happen. You can read more about how to get there in this book.

Maybe your parent is concerned about how you're eating and bought you this book, but you haven't talked to a doctor or medical professional yet. Or maybe you've already been diagnosed with a specific eating disorder and are in the middle of treatment. You might worry about food a lot but believe it's not "serious" enough to be an official disorder. Maybe you know you can't afford treatment, so you picked this book up instead.

This book will not cure you, but it *can* start you on the road to recovery. It can educate you about symptoms that you have and situations that you encounter as you work to become healthier and to develop a happier, more accepting relationship with your body.

That relationship is possible.

I promise.

# CHAPTER 2

## What Types of Treatment Are Available?

**DEPENDING ON YOUR** eating disorder symptoms, your medical needs, your need for weight gain, your financial status, whether you have insurance, and even where you live, treatment options will vary. But you do have options—many options, ranging from attending therapy sessions to staying in a hospital.

If you have insurance, it may cover therapy sessions, psychiatrist appointments, and medication. Your insurance may cover hospital stays. Sadly, though, many insurance companies deny coverage for some eating disorder treatments.

That's why it's important to realize that if you can't get one specific type of treatment, you aren't doomed. Quite the opposite! There are so many different kinds of help you can get—support *is* out there, regardless of your family's finances or your life situation.

Though a lot of media about eating disorders focuses on hospitalization, that isn't the only option. You can seek out individual or family therapy if you and your doctor agree that it seems right for you. If you aren't sure where to begin, a school counselor might be able to direct you to resources for therapy or help.

I've included information at the end of this book about hotlines you can call and websites you can visit to seek out help that may be more affordable. There are free support groups, therapists who offer sessions on a sliding scale based on your ability to pay, and scholarship funds for eating disorder treatment.

Help is out there. Here are some of the main types.

## Individual talk therapy

Therapists—who may be psychologists, counselors, or social workers—are medical professionals you can talk to. While all therapists will discuss your eating disorder symptoms in some way, they do have differences.

Some therapists will want to talk about your past in detail, to get a good idea of what led to your disordered eating. Therapists who practice psychodynamic therapy, a type of talk therapy, believe that as you talk about your past, you will come to see how it affects your current experiences, which will lead to self-knowledge and change.[5]

Other therapists will prefer to concentrate on what is going on now, on your behaviors and what leads to your actions. Cognitive behavioral therapy focuses on solving problems by concentrating on dysfunctional thoughts, emotions, and behaviors, then challenging those thoughts to change how you react.[6]

Therapists who use dialectical behavior therapy focus on painful emotions and behavior and teach skills to manage anxiety and negative thoughts.[7]

Mindfulness therapy, which was originally developed to use with depression, teaches how to deal with unwanted thoughts by accepting and becoming aware of them instead of immediately reacting and despairing.

If you have insurance, individual talk therapy is very likely covered, although you may be directed to certain providers in your network.

## Psychiatrists

Psychiatrists are medical professionals who can write prescriptions for medications that may help manage anxiety, depression, mood disorders, and other mental health issues that may be contributing to your eating disorder or body image issues.

## Family therapy

Family therapy usually occurs alongside individual therapy, often with a separate therapist altogether. Family therapy expands beyond talking about just *you* and your fears. Instead, it talks about the dynamic that exists around you and how the members of your family interact.

## Medical care

An important part of treatment, medical doctors can check on you and watch for physical complications that might come up during your recovery.

## Dietitians

Dietitians can help with meal plans and provide support to make sure that you're getting the right nutrition.

## Support groups

Often led by a professional therapist or a recovered individual, support groups involve a number of people getting together to talk about issues with disordered eating. Some support groups have a specific focus (anorexia, bulimia, binge eating, males with eating disorders, queer people, adults), while others are open to the general population. All focus on recovery. Moderators will be aware of triggers, the topics or comments that might tempt someone to return to disordered eating. Some groups will include a meal or snack during the meeting.

## Family-based treatment

In family-based treatment, also called the Maudsley approach, parents or guardians take an active role in helping their child recover through family meals. This type of treatment has proven very successful for kids and adolescents with supportive families.[8]

## Outpatient care

In outpatient care you continue to live at home but attend support groups or appointments with nutritionists, doctors, therapists, or psychiatrists who are affiliated with a hospital or an eating disorder support organization.

## Partial hospitalization

Partial hospitalization means you attend a hospital program for eating disorders, but still sleep at home. It is also called day treatment, since it usually runs from before breakfast until after dinner, most or all days of the week. Patients in day treatment still attend groups and meet with doctors in their program, but leave at the end of the day to practice coping skills at home.

## Inpatient care

Inpatient care means you stay in a hospital overnight as well as during the day. It is often used for people with medical problems that accompany their eating disorder. As with partial hospitalization, there are group and personal therapy sessions and a strict schedule.

## Residential care

Residential care is a long-term treatment where you live at a treatment center. It differs from inpatient care in that it is used for people who are medically stable. Therapists, counselors, and nutritionists are on staff, and the program works to ease you back into life with a lower level of care after discharge. These types of programs last anywhere from thirty to ninety days, sometimes longer, and are less likely to be covered by insurance, if you have it.

# How to find a therapist

As you look for a therapist, it's important to know that all therapists aren't alike. Some may prefer cognitive behavioral therapy, while some may want to dive into your past. Some may use a tough-love approach, while some may be more forgiving and gentle.

Above all, though, it's important to find a therapist who has experience treating eating disorders. This way, you know that the person you are opening yourself up to won't respond with an insensitive comment. They won't talk about your weight above all else. They are educated about eating disorders and will help give you the tools to fight them.

Eating disorder therapists come from a variety of backgrounds and can be psychologists, social workers, or licensed therapists. The National Eating Disorders Association website has a treatment finder where you, along with your parents or guardians, can enter your location and which eating disorders you are struggling with, along with any other conditions you might have and what kind of treatment you desire—not just inpatient, but also individual therapy and family therapy. *Psychology Today*'s Therapist Finder and Zocdoc can connect patients to therapists in their area, as can some of the organizations listed in the back of the book.

Another step in finding a therapist is to have your

parents or caregivers contact your insurance company. In the best-case scenario, therapy will be covered. This may mean that you have to pay a small co-pay for each appointment, but the bulk of the costs will be paid by your insurance company. Sometimes, insurance companies will tell you that you have to pick from a certain pool of therapists in order for them to pay. A lot of insurance companies let you search for therapists on their websites based on specific criteria, and you can also check to see if a certain provider will be covered.

If therapy isn't covered, some therapists do work with patients on a sliding scale of costs to make things more affordable. That usually means that they set a price based on your family's ability to pay. (There's also a section in the back of this book about different scholarship funds that can help families pay for treatment.)

Also remember that you don't have to hire the first therapist you meet. This person is working to help you, and that's why it's important to make sure that you are a good fit for each other. Ask questions about what you will do in your sessions. How long has the therapist been treating eating disorders? What marks progress? Will you get homework? How will parents or caregivers be involved? What will your sessions be like?

This is *your* therapist, *your* treatment, and *your* life. You deserve someone who works well with you.

For queer people, it's important to find a therapist or doctor who understands specific issues you may be dealing with. It's fine to ask health-care professionals whether they're trained in working with queer people and are sensitive to their needs and experiences.

Alithia Skye Zamantakis, author of the article "My Journey to Eating Disorder Treatment as Neither a Man or Woman,"[9] talked to me about their struggle to find a therapist.

"They assumed that I was a man by my voice. Then they assumed I was a woman," said Zamantakis, whose pronouns are *they/them*. "It's hard to explain gender when you're dealing with so much else. It made me feel that treatment wouldn't even work."[10]

Zamantakis is now working with a therapist who doesn't specialize in eating disorders but who is queer and understands more about the trans community.

The cost of therapy can also be a barrier to many people seeking treatment.

Michelle, a biology student who has struggled with restrictive disorders, struggled with the cost of therapy. Even with insurance, she said that her office visits to a psychiatrist tended to be expensive. However, she has been in talk therapy for about a year and a half and has found a therapeutic outlet in writing and bullet journaling. "It's been especially helpful in tracking my emotions, mental health, and thoughts," she said.[11]

Stephanie Covington Armstrong, author of the memoir *Not All Black Girls Know How to Eat: A Story of Bulimia*, spoke about how the way that society viewed her made the search for help difficult.

"Because I am black, people, doctors, friends assumed that black women do not have eating disorders because we are all born with an innate confidence about our body," she said. "I wore a mask of confidence to hide my issues with food and low self-esteem from those around me. Falling outside of the strong black woman archetype was not an option so I fed into the narrative that I could cope with any and all trauma myself. It was taboo to seek mental health support in my community so I stuck to the status quo and suffered in silence, using food to quell the inner voices of doubt and shame until I could no longer hide and had to step outside of my comfort zone and seek help."

Though Armstrong didn't receive eating-disorder-specific treatment, she was able to find help.

"I joined a twelve-step program for my food problems and sought help with a therapist," she said. "I really believe that real recovery can only come by working threefold: body, mind, and spirit."[12]

Twelve-step programs are like a support group but are made up entirely of people dealing with an unhealthy behavior or addiction (rather than being moderated by professionals). They involve a process that includes admitting powerlessness over an addiction or problem, believing that a higher power can help, working with an experienced sponsor to recognize past errors and make amends, and learning to live according to a new, healthier set of behaviors.

As you progress through recovery, you will continue to reevaluate the type of care that you need. At some points, you may choose to change the type of treatment that you are receiving. Sometimes, you may need a higher level of care. At other times, you may be doing well and need less support.

Above all, it is important to choose the path to recovery that works for you and your individual situation. Because whatever that path is, help is out there.

# PART TWO

Tools and Information
for Recovery

# CHAPTER 3
## Listening to Your Body

### Why is eating so hard?

**DISORDERED EATING IS** often all about ignoring hunger cues. A lot of recovery is learning to recognize when your body is telling you to eat, and learning to listen and respect those hunger cues. Dietitians and nutritionists can help you get back on track. They can calculate (approximately, not exactly) how many calories you'll need per day to maintain or gain weight, based on your height, weight, frame, and activity level. They'll work with you to develop a meal plan that includes certain ratios of certain food groups. They'll tell you how important it is to drink water and how fats are amazing at keeping your skin smooth and your hair shiny.

Meal plans aren't an exact science, but a dietitian can work with you and adjust a meal plan to be just right. Every human body is different. Even if two people have the exact same height and weight, they'll still need different amounts of food to stay healthy. Everyone has different metabolisms. Everyone lives their lives in different ways.

*Also*—and this can be the hardest part to understand, accept, and embrace—their bodies are meant to settle in different places, based on their genetics.

I get it. It stinks. Maybe you want to weigh less than you do right now. You may work hard to achieve that goal. You may actually change your weight for a while.

But what's the cost?

I know I probably sound as if I'm lecturing you. Every body is different, blah blah blah.

Maybe I *am* lecturing you, though, in the sense that I'm imparting information. But information isn't a bad thing. Information is what our bodies are trying to communicate to us every single day. Every minute. Every second.

Can you tell when your body is tired? When it needs sleep or rest? Can you tell when your body is hungry? Thirsty? Full? Can you tell when your emotions are intense or your good judgment is clouded?

Some people can. Some people can't. Some people exist on a continuum between these two states, understanding their body's messages only sometimes. The rest of the time they have no idea what is going on in the slightest.

Either that or they ignore the messages completely.

Where do you lie?

# What is intuitive eating?

In your recovery journey, you may hear about a concept called "intuitive eating," where the goal is to connect with your body's natural hunger and fullness cues. To eat when you are hungry and stop when you are full. To eat what you crave without judgment.[13]

Some people call this "normal" eating.

Here's the thing, though—I really hate the word *normal*. There *is* no "normal," especially when it comes to our society and food.

You may feel abnormal now because your relationship with food isn't the best. You may feel abnormal because you can't stop thinking about your body.

On the other hand, in today's world, aren't these disordered relationships and thoughts becoming more and more "normal"? Your mother may weigh herself every morning. Your best friends may skip lunch, and your brother may be on a diet to make weight for wrestling. When you turn on the TV or go to the movies, you don't see many plus-size actors and actresses. There are no fat Disney princesses. People go to the gym to "burn off Thanksgiving dinner" or run for hours to "earn that slice of birthday cake."

That's "normal" now, and it's all around us. So in a world where up is down and down is up and then down and then some other direction entirely, I think we should try to define our own "normal."

Society says that "normal" eating is organic foods, special diets, and "no carbs!"

Society says that "normal" eating is counting calories and trying to be small. Or trying to be toned and muscular. Society is loud.

Society yells so loudly that you can't hear yourself.

Society is wrong.

Here's what "normal" eating is, as defined in 1983 by dietitian Ellyn Satter, an authority on eating and feeding. The Ellyn Satter Institute counsels and trains both nutrition professionals and the public on how to eat with joy. Among its guidelines are eating when hungry and stopping when satisfied, eating foods you like, and considering nutrition while not restricting your diet. It emphasizes trusting your body and realizing that normal eating is flexible, rather than rigid.

I like this definition of "normal" way better than how many people define it. With this definition, you don't have to be a robot, making exactly sure that calories in equal calories out. Because let me tell you, trying to figure out exactly what your body wants is hard. Really hard. It's stressful and confusing and can really tap into the perfectionist streak that so many of us have.

What I like the most about Satter's definition is that food isn't only talked about in terms of energy and hunger. Food is discussed in terms of feelings, too. Because sometimes, when you're sad, a snack *may* make you feel better.

A snack isn't the *only* thing that could make you feel better, of course. Crying or talking to a friend or blaring music or writing in your journal or getting lost in a book or punching the air furiously while kickboxing might help, too.

Food is so many different things to so many different people.

Some people see food as something to consume to give them energy. Some people see food as a way to connect with loved ones.

Other people look at food as a way to classify themselves as superior to others, thinking that they're "healthier" because of their diet. They may see food as a way to judge themselves, and beat themselves up for having a snack.

But it's just a snack. Seriously. And if that snack is going to make you feel good in the moment after a hideous day, then have it and move on. Don't give it another thought.

That's the hard part, though. The "don't give it another thought" part. That's why you're reading this book. Because you *do* think about things like that. You think about things like that a lot. So did I, both when I was sick and when I was trying to recover and understand my body for the first time.

Recovery isn't easy. It's the hardest thing I've ever done. But it started with my body. It started with me listening to what my body needed *and* to what my body wanted. It started with me not being a robot, but being a human. One who makes mistakes and has too much food sometimes and too little food at other times.

We are all different. We have different homes and different friends. We have different family structures. Eventually, we'll have different careers and different lives. We don't all have the same foot size. We don't all have the same body size, either.

Your body will tell you what size it wants to be if you listen to it. Not all the time, not exactly, but most of the time.

For those in early recovery, intuitive eating is not recommended right away. It takes your body some time to heal from the damage you've inflicted. It takes time for it to trust you again. So at first, intuitive eating may be replaced by a meal plan set up by a nutritionist. It may be replaced by a certain number of meals and snacks per day.

But over time, your body will learn to trust you. You can choose to follow your stomach and your brain without worrying about how those choices will affect your body. You can do what you want. You can eat what you need.

# EXERCISE: ARE YOU HUNGRY?

The next time you're hungry or full or tired, listen to the messages you start telling yourself (or start telling your body). Write them down.

Examples:

I just ate. I shouldn't be hungry.
I ate so much. I'm an awful person.
I'm tired, but I should go for a run.
Why am I so tired? I'm so lazy.

Are these things you're telling yourself true? These are all examples of what I call the "eating disorder voice," which we'll talk about in a later chapter. How is that voice making you feel? Why is it trying to make you ignore your body's signals?

# CHAPTER 4

## Nutrition: It's More Than Just Food Groups

### What is healthy eating?

**EVEN THOUGH IT'S** important to listen to our body's signals, that's not an excuse to forget about good nutrition. And I know—believe me I know—disordered eaters will use any excuse to forget about good nutrition.

I'm not advocating for a life with perfect nutritional habits. Perfect nutritional habits are just another manifestation of an eating disorder, and for those struggling with orthorexia, the obsession with "clean" eating, a focus on ideal nutrition can do more harm than good.

"Clean" eating sounds like a good thing. It's the opposite of dirty, after all. And if being clean is good, that must mean that *we're* good, too. Right?

But "clean" eating is restrictive. It means analyzing

nutrition labels and obsessing about organic foods and additives. It's the opposite of balance.

As I was writing this book, I spoke with Lori Lieberman, a registered dietitian who specializes in eating disorders. Lieberman mentioned that one of the mistakes her clients make is trying to micromanage their food: "We think if a cupcake doesn't have nutrients like protein or fiber, then it's junk. But we don't have to get all of our nutrients from a single item. We don't eat single foods. Within the context of a healthy diet there is room for cupcakes."[14]

We don't have to eat "clean" all the time to get our nutrients. We don't have to eat all healthy foods all the time to fuel our bodies. Instead, we need to think big picture. Desserts can be part of a healthy diet, as long as our vitamin and food group needs are being met elsewhere.

We're allowed to eat processed foods, like store-bought desserts. We're allowed to eat fruits and vegetables, too. That's what I mean by good nutrition, and that's what balance is: a little of this and a little of that. Balance comes from strengthening and energizing your body with a variety of food groups while still allowing yourself to enjoy food and live a life that makes your taste buds dance.

(It is also pretty fun to imagine taste buds dancing.)

One of the first things all my treatment providers made me do when I was first diagnosed with an eating disorder was to give them a list of what I ate in a normal day.

I lied, of course. Partially because I was embarrassed of what they would think of me and partially because I knew that if I told them, they would make me eat more. And at that point, I didn't want to stop what I was doing. Not yet.

(I still made the real list of food I ate in my head, though. I still realized, deep down, that I wasn't eating enough. That I was hungry more often than not. That something was wrong.)

One thing that's pretty amazing is to watch a little kid eat. Kids get hungry. They whine and cry and ask for food. They ask for exactly what they want:

"Can I have a snack?"

"I'm still hungry."

"I'm done. I'm full."

Kids are incredible when it comes to listening to their bodies. To hearing and obeying their hunger cues. Kids leave a spoonful of food in the bowl because their bellies are starting to hurt. They eat an entire container of blueberries because they're delicious and they've been outside all morning.

Usually, kids eat three meals, along with two or three snacks. This is the schedule a nutritionist will probably put you on when you start recovery from an eating disorder. When I entered treatment, the meal schedule was extremely strict: breakfast, snack, lunch, snack, dinner, snack. It was the same thing every day, at the exact same time.

If you are currently in a treatment program or seeing a nutritionist, this is most likely the schedule you follow, too. In fact, Lieberman stressed how important it is *not* to try intuitive eating early in your recovery since all the chaos going on in your body and brain (such as eating disorder thoughts, anxiety, and suppressed hunger from slowed metabolic rate, for those who are restricting calories) will interfere with your body's signals. You may be so anxious that it will be hard to listen to your body. That's why meal plans—specific words on paper for you to follow—are so important.

Meal plans will change over time. In recovery, your metabolism (which controls how fast your body uses calories and how often you get hungry) is always shifting. But the plan's structure is important. That structure will remind your body that you are fueling it and that you will *continue* to fuel it.

## Chronic illness and eating disorders

Chronic illnesses can also complicate a healthy relationship with food. Chronic illnesses are long-term or lifelong illnesses that can disrupt your life in many ways and that generally require a lot of time and energy to manage. Many chronic illnesses are incurable, and treatment may just be focused on managing symptoms, which can be a source of frustration, anger, and anxiety. Chronic illnesses are also often managed with strict diets, which can lead to a preoccupation with food and "health."

Examples of chronic illness include cancer, cystic fibrosis, chronic pain, Crohn's disease and ulcerative colitis, diabetes, celiac disease, migraines, and insomnia/narcolepsy, though there are many more.

People with certain chronic conditions also may have a hard time with body image and recovery. People with chronic illnesses like Crohn's, diabetes, or celiac disease may have to avoid certain foods, and many health-care practitioners may even suggest restrictive meal plans that are thought to help the symptoms of the chronic illness. The problem with these meal plans is that if people are already hyperconscious of their bodies, their eating habits, and their health, this focus on food can turn obsessive.

Sarah M. talked to me about her struggle to recover from an eating disorder after her diagnosis of type 2 diabetes: "I find that I'm even more obsessed with food sometimes because I'm trying to hit blood sugar goals and count calories, sugar, and carbs," she said.[15] Sarah said that because of her diabetes, she sometimes has to eat foods different from the ones she actually wants, which can interfere with the recovery goal of eating a variety of foods.

Some chronic gastrointestinal illnesses like Crohn's can make people lose weight when they're sick and gain weight when they're healthy. Strangers—or even loved ones—

may make comments about a person's weight or body changes, implying that they looked better when they were at a lower weight, even if that meant they were extremely sick. These comments can trigger unhealthy thoughts and assumptions in the minds of those already focused on their bodies.

Chronic illnesses don't only complicate and trigger eating disorders. Their symptoms might also *mask* eating disorders. Some people with eating disorders explain away their weight loss by blaming it on their physical disease. I spoke with one woman whose disordered eating was overlooked because others concentrated more on the physical symptoms that were going on at the same time: the stomach ulcer and acid reflux that made eating painful.

People with type 1 diabetes often lose weight before their disease is discovered.[16] After starting insulin treatment, though, the body can return to a higher, healthier weight. One person who was recently diagnosed with type 1 diabetes talked to me about the psychological difficulties that came with accepting this higher weight, especially after she had received compliments from others on her previous weight loss.

Type 1 diabetes is often diagnosed in adolescence, the same time that body image concerns start to take hold. It doesn't seem coincidental that girls with type 1 diabetes are

2.4 times more likely to develop an eating disorder than those without diabetes.[17]

Luckily, nutritionists take chronic illnesses, along with multiple other factors, into consideration when creating meal plans for people suffering from eating disorders.

## Who are nutritionists?

Nutritionists are professionals who can create a meal plan based on your age, height, and level of activity. They can tell you how much to eat and the ideal eating times for you. They can tell you how much and what kind of activities you can do for exercise. If you're an athlete, your caloric needs will be higher because of your physical activity. The nutritionist will change your meal plan according to how your body reacts.

If you're seeing a nutritionist, you may hate your meal plan. You may want to disobey your nutritionist. A nutritionist may make a lot of suggestions that seem obvious, even annoying.

Of course, you know you need to eat healthy food in healthy amounts! *Obviously* you know all these things. You hate worrying so much about your body or food.

Knowing what to do isn't the same as doing it, though. That's what makes an eating disorder an eating disorder. Knowing the steps to take to recover isn't the same as actually taking them. That's why, if it's financially feasible, meeting with a professional nutritionist to talk things out can be helpful. It's one extra support on your journey, and that's never a bad thing.

## Fat isn't bad

Many of us have been taught to think that being fat is a bad thing and that to be fat, or to become fat, is bad. Those messages are wrong.

As I mentioned earlier, fat is not bad. Saying that someone is fat is not a moral judgment. Fatness is not a sin. Fat is a term for describing bodies, like "tall" or "blond" or "freckled," and while the term should be neutral, it has become loaded and used as a weapon. "Fat" isn't the only term that has been weaponized to harm people; "obese" is a medical term that many people—including doctors and other health-care professionals—pull out when they want to justify discrimination against fat people.

A person can be fat and healthy. In fact, it can be much more dangerous to be thin than fat. A 2016 study of almost fifty thousand women and five thousand men age forty and older in the Canadian province of Manitoba showed that the skinniest women in the experimental group, those who were considered "underweight" or "normal weight," had a 44 percent higher risk of dying during the following seven years, while "overweight" participants had the best chance of survival.[18]

The Health at Every Size movement exists to show people that you can, in fact, be healthy at any size and that dieting actually doesn't work.[19] When you restrict your food, your brain thinks about eating more. Your metabolism changes so you need fewer calories to survive. Dieting makes you hungrier, which can lead to eating more than you're actually hungry for.

Your body is meant to stay within its unique size range. When you diet in order to break out of this range, your body will fight back. That's why it's so important for you *not* to push back at your body. Continuing to start and restart diets can actually cause health problems, and many of these illnesses are the ones attributed to the so-called "obesity epidemic"!

For example, in a 2016 Everyday Feminism article co-written with Melissa A. Fabello, professor, researcher, and *Health at Every Size* author Dr. Bacon noted that constant dieting can cause inflammation in the body. But then—surprise!—the effects of that inflammation (diabetes, heart disease, etc.) are blamed on "obesity."[20]

(I'll talk later about how the body mass index and the labels "overweight" and "obese" don't necessarily reveal anything about your *real* health.)

That's why it's important to figure out how your relationship with food really makes you feel and why it's so helpful to work with a professional. A nutritionist can help you eat more healthily. A nutritionist and meal plan can help your body *be* healthy and function the way it's supposed to, regardless of your size.

Sometimes getting healthier might involve gaining weight. Sometimes it might involve unintentionally losing weight as a result of being more active or learning to eat based on hunger cues. But here's the thing to keep in mind: Weight gain does not equal a failure. Weight loss does not equal a victory.

The true victory is finding the weight that is healthiest for you. It's different for everyone and can change at every stage of life. A healthy weight can mean being fat. And that's 100 percent okay.

## You can retrain your body to eat regularly again

Before you can trust your body to know what it wants, you need to teach it how to eat regularly again. You need to reassure your body that you won't continue hurting it with your eating disorder. For so many of us, these behaviors are all our bodies know.

Our bodies are smart. When they're treated a certain way, they compensate. They fight back. Our bodies want to live. They want to protect us.

For example, if you give your body too little food, it will

slow down your metabolism. Your body will never know when it will be fed, so it will hang on to every calorie. Bodies want food because they're programmed for survival. Bodies will *tell* you that they want food.

But first you have to show your body that you're eating regularly again.

One of the main goals of a meal plan is to prove to your body that it *will* be getting food on a regular basis. To show your body that it can start to digest and metabolize food as it is supposed to. To communicate that it can trust you again. Because just as you may not trust your body to stabilize at a place where you "approve" of its shape and its weight, your body doesn't trust you, either. You don't have a history of taking care of it.

I certainly didn't take care of my body. Even when I decided to recover, I still didn't know what my body needed. I was used to being sick with my eating disorder. I was used to comparing nutrition labels. I was used to ignoring my needs. I needed help.

Lieberman said that she helps her clients recognize that they need a *range* of foods, not only to meet their nutrient needs, but also to satisfy. "Eating 'healthy' foods doesn't equal healthy eating," she told me. "You can eat lots of wholesome foods and not eat enough or still miss out on many nutrients. You need to allow yourself the pleasure of food, too."[21]

# Refeeding syndrome and dealing with discomfort

If your body hurts, it may make you want to stop this whole recovery thing. This is especially true when you realize how physically uncomfortable it can be to start eating "normally" after you've stuffed or starved your body for so long. This physical discomfort *does* happen, although in varying degrees depending on your history of disordered eating.

I spoke with Dr. Mariela Podolski, the Medical Director of the Inpatient Unit of Walden Behavior Care in Rockville, Connecticut, who stressed the difference between an official condition called "refeeding syndrome" and the refeeding pains that many people experience in recovery.[22]

Refeeding pains refer to the discomfort that your body goes through as you start taking in more food on a regular schedule of eating. Because your eating patterns have been so erratic and disordered, you may be bloated and uncomfortable as you start eating more food. You may always feel full or even nauseous.

These are feelings that will pass, though. Your stomach and your gastrointestinal tract—a passage that goes from the mouth throughout your body—are not used to you taking care of your body and listening to your hunger pains. They need time to grow stronger and to adjust.

Dr. Podolski told me that the GI tract is a muscle, and likened the refeeding process to someone beginning a running program for the first time. After that first day of running, you might be sore the next morning. You will probably be sore the second and third day of running, too.

"Do you stop?" asked Dr. Podolski. "No. You'll be sore for a while, but as you keep training, your muscles get stronger and you're not sore anymore. Just like the muscles in your legs, your GI tract is a muscle, too, and you need to condition it to be stronger."

The way to do that is by continuing to eat and to push past the "soreness," in this case the bloating, the discomfort, and those feelings of fullness.

Refeeding syndrome is different, though, and Dr. Podolski stressed how dangerous this condition can be, along with how it is one of the major causes of death once a severely malnourished person (of any weight) starts eating regularly again.

When you starve yourself for a specific period of time, even for as little as five to ten days, according to Dr. Podolski, your body doesn't receive the nutrients that it needs from food. Since the nutrients aren't coming in, your body will pull from its reserves instead. Phosphorus is one of these important nutrients, and one of its roles is to manage and store energy in the body.

When you start eating again during the refeeding process, your body's needs shift. All of a sudden, it wants more and more phosphorus. But since you don't have any reserves left, your body's levels will drop.

And that is the dangerous part. That shock to your body is what causes refeeding syndrome, which can lead to heart failure, cardiac arrhythmia (abnormal heart rhythms), swelling, and even death.

Refeeding syndrome does not happen to everyone who starts eating again. But it can happen. And the more weight you lose, the more likely it is to happen.

Hypoglycemia, or low blood sugar, can also be a danger factor for those who have been restricting their intake. People who have been malnourished for a long time eventually get used to having low blood sugar. Even with incredibly low levels, they may say they feel "fine."

Except this means that there are no warning signs when blood sugar levels drop even more, which can lead to further medical complications and even death.

Eating disorders are scary, and not just while you're engaging in eating disordered behaviors. These behaviors can affect your recovery, too, and that's why it's so necessary to stop them now. Not later, but now, before you reach that danger zone.

That's why it's also so important to follow a meal plan under a nutritionist's and medical provider's care, especially if you are severely underweight or have lost a significant amount of weight. When dramatic changes happen to your body all at once, it can be dangerous.

Please don't let these side effects and potential complications scare you off. Staying sick is always worse than aiming for recovery, and the finishing line of recovery will outweigh any momentary uncomfortable and/or gross parts of the process (especially if you are appropriately monitored).

And recovery can be gross.

You may fart a lot. You may be constipated. Your stomach can cramp up and look so bloated you appear to be carrying a baby in there. You could burp a lot. You might feel full after half a sandwich because your stomach has shrunk so much. You may feel like you have to throw up.

Fun, huh?

Your refeeding pains won't last forever, though. As your body adjusts, the symptoms will ease and lessen. Your body will get used to working and metabolizing food the way it's supposed to. Your GI tract will strengthen. You will start to get hungry and full. You will start to recognize when you're hungry and full.

Little by little, and with the help of medical professionals, your body will begin to stabilize and trust you. You will learn to live—to eat—in a way that honors and satisfies your mind and your body, and that helps you be as healthy as you're able to be.

**NOTE**: If you don't have insurance and are worried about not being able to afford the medical care you need, there are treatment scholarships you can apply for, and some academic hospitals provide treatment to those willing to participate in a research trial. If you're underage, ask your parent or guardian to look into options in your area. If you *have* insurance but it denies you coverage, there's still hope: Many individuals and families whose insurance denies care end up petitioning their insurance company for coverage in these cases.

# CHAPTER 5
## Self-Esteem, or "What's Good About Me?"

### How I struggled with self-esteem

**WHEN I HAD** an eating disorder, that eating disorder became part of my identity. It became what was good about me. I was good at losing weight. I could eat less than all my friends.

I was good at exercising. I thought I exercised better than anyone else. I was good at being skinny. People complimented me on my weight loss. People said they wanted to be like me.

It was the first time that anyone said they wanted to be like me.

When I was a kid, my brothers were good at sports. Really good. "Made two varsity teams as freshmen" good.

I was okay at swimming, but only made the B team.

I got stuck in the chorus when the school musical was cast.

I was good at school but was never the absolute best in my class.

I was good at reading, but you couldn't exactly say you wanted to be a reader someday.

Then I started losing weight.

It started off innocently enough. It was just a little diet. I learned all the rules to get in shape. I followed those rules. I exercised a certain amount and ate what I was "supposed" to. I lost weight. I started getting compliments.

I felt like a celebrity on the red carpet, with reporters and fans shouting words of praise at me, pushing to take pictures, wanting to be me and asking for my secrets.

For the first time, I *had* secrets. I had what I believed was a *talent*. For once in my life, I was good at something. I was the *best* at something, and I wasn't going to let anyone take that away from me.

For me, casting off this identity was one of the hardest parts of recovery. After years of starving and restricting, my eating disorder wasn't just a collection of behaviors anymore: It was who I was. Getting rid of that identity— stopping all related behaviors and letting go of the pride associated with being sick or "skinny"—is a difficult task, especially in a society where thinness is seen as a virtue.

For a long time, I didn't think I *was* good at anything else. I wasn't even good at *recovery* for a long time. I cheated on my meal plan and lied in therapy.

I tried to hang on to my eating disorder—my identity—

for as long as I could because it still made me feel special. I thought it was all that I had.

## Why being thin couldn't be the good thing about me

After years of trying to hold on to my eating disorder, I couldn't do it anymore. I was too sad, too tired, and too hungry to keep doing everything that kept me sick. Losing weight got harder, too.

Despite what a lot of media says about weight loss, the more you try to lose weight, the harder it becomes. Many people don't realize that weight loss is not necessarily a matter of "calories in versus calories out." Studies have shown that people's hormones actually change after they go on restrictive diets. A 2016 study looking at the effects of television's *The Biggest Loser* found that the restrictive diets the contestants had been put on caused their metabolisms to slow down.[23] In fact, their metabolisms were still slow *six whole years* after they had left the show! Though they had lost weight over the course of the show, that weight loss wasn't permanent for most contestants, through no fault of their own. The act of weight loss made their bodies adjust, so their bodies needed less food to maintain their weight.

The body doesn't like being on a strict diet. The body

wants to stay within its own weight range. It fights back when you fight against it. That's what happened to me as my eating disorder continued. Losing weight became harder. I became more and more miserable.

Finally, I realized how much of my life I was missing out on. My friends were having fun and moving forward without me. I wanted what they had. I wanted to change. I wanted to recover.

So I started to do things a bit differently. I ate more. I listened to what my therapist said. I tried to sit with the discomfort that I was feeling.

## The scale doesn't dictate your self-worth

I threw out my scale, too. This was a hard decision to make. For many people struggling with disordered eating, the scale feels like an important—even a vital—part of their life. At that point in my life, the scale felt like my friend. Seeing that number was something that I could count on. I didn't know what my life would look like if I couldn't have that stability every day.

Here's the thing, though: The scale *didn't* give me stability. In fact, the scale was more like a dictator than a friend. It told me what to do and how to feel based on the number that flashed on its display. It took away my peace of mind, my spontaneity, and my freedom.

Without the scale, I thought I'd feel lost.

But I also knew that without the scale, I could dictate my moods. I could decide whether or not I was sad or happy at a certain moment—not because of my weight but because of whatever else was going on in my life.

This simple action helped my recovery immensely. At first, it produced anxiety. I kept imagining awful things happening to my body. How would I know what to fix if I didn't have that number? But over time, not weighing myself got easier. I realized that I didn't necessarily have to fix *anything*, and the urge to step on the machine lessened. Because that's all the scale is—a machine. A machine that you don't *need* to own or use.

Sometimes, instead of throwing away their scales, some people hold scale-smashing parties, hitting it with a hammer until its insides are exposed as nothing more than metal parts. (This should not be done without adult supervision.) Some people decorate their scales and replace the numbers with affirmations.

Depending on who you live with, you may not be able to transform or get rid of your scale. Parents or caregivers might like to weigh themselves. They may resist your suggestion to throw it out. In this case, you can choose to avoid the scale. You can try to remember that you do not need the information it gives you.

That information says nothing about you as a person. It

says nothing about how you treat other people or what you enjoy doing.

It says nothing about how amazing you are, regardless of the size or shape of your body.

## Why finding joy is so hard

"Enjoy life." It sounds so easy, doesn't it? Aren't humans wired to have fun?

Some people are, but some people are naturally more anxious. Some people are extroverts and love being around other people—while others are introverts and need quiet alone time to recharge.

Some people have life circumstances or a financial situation that makes it harder to have fun. Some may still encounter bullying or discrimination as they try to recover.

Even if you have a positive support network surrounding you, the early days of recovery will probably not involve you bouncing around the room and hanging out with your friends every day. Recovery is a long road. It takes a long time to find yourself. And a lot of that time will involve worry and fear.

I am a natural worrier. And for me, recovery led to way more anxiety at first. I was worried that I still thought about food. I was worried about my weight gain. I was worried that I didn't actually know what I liked. After all, I'd ignored everything but my body for years. I was so used to going through life with a one-track mind that it was almost impossible to think about what brought me joy. I didn't know what true joy was anymore or what I should want, both for my body and for my life.

## How I found a way to feel happier

There's a saying that tells us to "enjoy the journey instead of focusing on the destination." If we're driving cross country, we'll miss out on all the gorgeous views out the window if we keep worrying about when we're going to get there. Life isn't just the end result; life is what comes between Point A and Point B.

You can look at fun the same way. You don't have to be awesome at something to enjoy it. You don't have to always do something just to win the gold medal or the blue ribbon. You can do it because it makes you smile or gets your mind off something you're worried about.

"Journey" activities are just as important as "destination" activities. And during my recovery, it was important that journey activities had nothing to do with my body, eating, or exercise. I had to learn to have fun outside of these areas of self-worth and "achievement."

At first, I could only think of two things I liked to do that didn't involve my body: read and watch TV.

*Boring!* I yelled at myself. *What kind of person has fun*

*just reading and watching TV? Where's the excitement in that? Where's the struggle? Where's the glory?*

I had to keep reminding myself that I wasn't striving for what I thought of as "glory" anymore. I didn't want "victory," or what my eating disorder had told me was victory. To my eating disorder, success was losing so much weight that I landed in the hospital. My disease wanted to hand me a gold medal as I was lying in a coffin.

Your disease wants that, too.

I don't want that for you, though. I want you to want more for yourself, too. I want you to stop entering races and racking up the blue ribbons. You don't have to be a professional all the time. You can be an amateur, too. You can have a hobby.

You don't always have to win.

I read a lot when I first started recovering. I watched TV a lot, too. I tried knitting and crocheting, but I got bored fast. I tried a lot of activities I thought I *should* like until I settled on ones I *did* like.

Here are some of the activities that truly brought me joy:

- Reading
- Watching TV
- Baking cookies
- Going to the beach
- Doing crossword puzzles
- Swimming
- Playing piano

The list was still short, and I still thought it was boring. I told myself that no one ever became special by going to the beach or doing crossword puzzles. And I wasn't all that great at piano. But I had to learn that I was special the way I was and that even the little things that brought me joy were important.

Even though I wasn't all that good at piano, playing and knowing I was improving made me feel happier than my eating disorder had. Even though these things were "minor," they made me feel good about myself.

You may have heard the phrase "you are not your body." If so, you probably roll your eyes and groan when you hear it. It's a cliché, but it's true, too. The people who love you, or who *will* love you, care because of who you are, not because of what you look like. They're not lying when they say that. There's no camera and film crew waiting to film your shock and horror as everyone shouts that this was all a huge trick.

You *aren't* your body. You *are* your smile and your interests and your passions. If you're passionate about television, watch television! Talk about your favorite shows with your friends! Join a fandom, draw fan art. Read and write fan fiction and go to cons. Dream up your own television show and write episodes!

If you like to swim, swim! You don't have to join a team or qualify for the Olympics. Feel your body glide through the water. Strap a pair of goggles on and do laps. Play Marco Polo with your friends on a hot summer day. Swim across a lake and have a picnic afterward.

If you like music, try an instrument! Play it even if you're bad, even if it takes you forever to learn the simplest song. You can listen to music. Sing at the top of your lungs in the car, even if you sound like a frog gargling water.

Find people who have the same interests as you and talk about them. Do things together. Being with other people is so much more fulfilling than being alone with your body. Especially when you spend all your time abusing and berating it. And if you want to be alone, embrace that, too. Solitude—when you're not spending the whole time unhappy with yourself—can be wonderful.

Once I started enjoying things, my life expanded. I became more than what my body looked like. I became Jen who loves reading stories with happily ever afters. I became Jen who likes country music. I became Jen who lives a life without always striving to be the best—and enjoys that life anyway.

In the process, I learned how to have fun. I learned how to love myself.

You can, too.

## EXERCISE: FINDING CONTENTMENT AND JOY

Make a list of things that you enjoy doing. (These should be things *you* like doing. Not things that your *friends* like to do and not things your parent or guardian thinks you should do.) If the list is short, that's okay. Focus on one of these things and make an effort to do that activity sometime during the next week without focusing on achievement. How does this make you feel?

You can keep revisiting this list over time, as you think of new things you'd like to do and try.

## EXERCISE: WHAT DO YOU WANT TO ACCOMPLISH AND LEARN?

Make a list of your accomplishments, knowledge, or talents that have nothing to do with your eating disorder, body, or how other people see you. Then make a list of other things you'd like to accomplish or learn.

# CHAPTER 6

## What Is Anxiety?

### Anxiety and learning to trust your body

**SOMETIMES TRUSTING YOUR** body will make it easier to eat more food and stop when you are full. Sometimes thinking about your awesome qualities will help you stop comparing your body. But sometimes—lots of times—it's *hard* to trust your body. Maybe you just ate a huge meal and can't think of a single thing that's good about you. Maybe someone made a comment that your body looks different.

Maybe you don't feel comfortable in your own skin. Maybe you're anxious about something else in your life, like school, friends, or family. In fact, these nonfood-related anxieties can affect your mental health just as much as the fears that go along with food and your body.

One thing I heard over and over in treatment was that eating disorders are "not about food."

"Yeah, right," I answered. "Of *course* they're about food. Can't you see that I have a problem with eating?" What I didn't realize or admit, for way too long, was that these professionals were right. My problems *weren't* just about food.

Food is food. Food is fuel. Food should be neutral. It was my fears about being accepted and being "perfect" that were causing that anxiety.

Anxieties can feed into other anxieties. If you're nervous about money or parent problems, if you're being bullied or having trouble in school, you may use eating disorder behaviors to distract yourself from what's really going on.

You may also be genetically wired to be anxious. For many, there is no "logical" reason to feel so on edge. Yet they are. And these feelings are just as valid.

So what do you do when you start feeling anxious? When someone says that you look "healthier," do you automatically translate that to "you look fat"? Do you get angry at your body for being a different size and shape from what you want it to be? Do you do something that will hurt you in the long run? Anxiety is awful. When I get anxious, I feel it throughout my body. My chest tightens, and my muscles tense. My heart beats faster, and my breath comes more quickly. Every inch of my skin feels alive and constricting.

Everyone manifests anxiety in different ways. Some

people perspire. Some people have full-blown panic attacks, which can feel more like heart attacks. Symptoms of a panic attack include feelings of fear or danger, dizziness, shortness of breath, heart palpitations, weakness, numbness or tingling, hot or cold flashes, sweating, and chest pressure.[24] Some people take medication to ease their anxiety symptoms. Some do deep breathing or yoga or wait it out.

Some don't know how to deal at all and cope by hurting themselves instead.

## Fight, flight, or freeze, and why we feel anxiety

We can panic when we encounter a situation that is unknown to us because the unknown can feel like a threat. In a situation like this, we have three options: fight, flight, or freeze.[25]

Animals have similar reactions when they are faced with threats to their survival. Their sympathetic nervous system releases hormones that get them ready for action.[26] When animals are threatened, they are instantly alert. The process is automatic and subconscious to ensure survival—without a thought, animals are ready to fight or flee.

Human beings are animals, too, and while we might not face the same threats as mountain lions in the wild, our bodies work in similar ways. When we face a threat, our bodies react. Our heart rate may pick up. We may get pale or flushed. Our blood vessels and pupils dilate, and our body shakes. Digestion may be affected.

We're not mountain lions, though. Our daily anxieties aren't the same as those of animals fighting for their lives in the wild. Our worst-case scenario usually isn't death.

It can feel just as dire, though, especially for those with eating disorders or low self-esteem. When someone calls you a name and your heart starts beating faster, it can feel as if you really might die. You may want to run away.

A lot of times, your way of escaping this feeling will be to do exactly what your eating disorder wants you to do. Your eating disorder is a coping mechanism, a way of soothing and distracting yourself from the real problem. These obsessions and harmful behaviors are your disorder's version of "fight or flight."

In the short term, falling back on your eating disorder might make your anxiety feel easier to cope with. But then what? What happens after, when you still haven't dealt with the initial threat, issue, or encounter that hurt you? What happens the next time you face the problem and you still don't know how to solve it?

You'll be even more tempted to turn to your eating disorder again and again.

That's how the cycle continues. That's how people get sick and stay sick. Anxiety feeds off itself. The more you indulge it and turn to harmful coping mechanisms, the stronger it returns. You need to *face* anxiety—to *tolerate* anxiety—to learn how to deal with it and gradually lessen its place in your life.

That's the hard part. That's the awful part. But there are techniques that can help.

## The diversity of people's brains and eating disorders

Most people experience anxiety at one time or another, but some people also deal with anxiety or challenges that are related to other specific conditions.

Though much of society is set up for people whose brains work in one particular way, there's huge variety in the ways brains work. That variety is called "neurodiversity."

"Neurotypical" describes anyone whose mind works in the way that society is set up for.

"Neurodivergent" or "non-neurotypical" describes anyone whose mind differs from the type the world is set up for. For example, autistic people, people with some mental illnesses, and people with attention deficit hyperactivity disorder (ADHD) or dyslexia are generally considered neurodivergent.[27]

What does this look like in daily life? For example, the loud noise of an automatic hand dryer might not bother a neurotypical person, but to someone who's bothered by unexpected loud noises, like many autistic people, that sound can be unbearable.

When it comes to eating disorders, neurodivergent people face their own unique set of challenges, particularly because they might already face challenges with a world that isn't set up to accommodate them.

One type of neurodivergence is autism spectrum disorder, where people have difficulty with social skills, sensory processing, speech, and nonverbal communication, among other things.[28]

I spoke to writer Rachel Simon, who is on the spectrum and was diagnosed as anorexic with avoidant restrictive food intake disorder tendencies.[29] This diagnosis often overlaps with autism, as both disorders can involve a sensitivity to the texture and smell of certain foods. For Simon, her eating disorder wasn't so much a desire to lose weight, but a lack of desire to eat. Eating was a chore. She didn't care. Often, eating certain foods disgusted her.

Katie Linden, a mental health counselor who was diagnosed as autistic when she was thirty-one, told me how her eating disorder started as a result of accidentally skipping breakfast one morning because she was late for school.

"By lunchtime, I had discovered that being hungry made all of my anxiety disappear—I felt kind of numb and floaty, and I was distracted from the abuse and isolation going on around me. After that, I started trying to restrict so I could feel like that all of the time."[30]

It wasn't until Linden's diagnosis years later that she realized that much of her rigidity, anxiety, and obsession with detail had to do with being autistic, not just having an eating disorder.

Intense, excessive feelings of anxiety that don't go away can be their own disorder, though, and can exacerbate an eating disorder.

There are many different types of anxiety disorders, but all involve a persistent, serious feeling of worry and fear. This isn't a basic, occasional feeling of nervousness or uncertainty over a test. This feeling is not temporary and often gets worse over time. Anxiety disorders stop people from living their lives and affect their behavior in school or with friends.

Anxiety disorders can include panic attacks, which are different for everyone, but often involve a combination of physical symptoms (racing heart, nausea, churning stomach, sweating) and snowballing thoughts (*I'm having a heart attack; this is never going to end; am I dying?*).

Some anxiety disorders, like generalized anxiety disorder, involve anxiety extending to various aspects of your life.[31] Others, like social anxiety disorder, can be focused on specific situations, like speaking in public, meeting new people, or returning to a specific place or circumstance in which you previously suffered embarrassment.[32]

What to keep in mind about all anxiety disorders is that they:

    1. are not your fault,

    2. interfere with your life,

    3. can make anxiety around food worse.

Obsessive-compulsive disorder is an anxiety disorder where the sufferer has both obsessions (repeated thoughts or images that cause anxiety) and compulsions (an urge to repeat a behavior to relieve the anxiety).[33]

Common obsessions include fear of germs, fear of death, fear of being violent, and the need for things to be perfectly neat and symmetrical.

Common compulsions include washing hands, arranging and ordering things, excessive cleaning or counting, and checking to make sure things are a certain way.

However, obsessions and compulsions are different in everyone. People with OCD can also have intrusive thoughts, which are scary or disturbing and come up automatically.

I myself have been diagnosed with obsessive-compulsive disorder, which was a huge factor in my anorexia. With OCD, the mind fixates on something, and the nervous system believes danger is imminent if the person doesn't complete a certain action. For me, I had to eat a certain way and exercise a certain number of minutes. If I didn't, I would feel that sense of anxiety and impending doom. The only way I could relieve it was to perform that compulsion.

Anxiety is just one of the many mental health conditions that can exist alongside an eating disorder.

People with post-traumatic stress disorder can have eating disorders. PTSD is a condition of extreme stress or anxiety following a traumatic event or the threat of a traumatic event.[34] While often talked about in terms of soldiers returning from war, PTSD can affect anyone who lives through an awful event. In fact, the event only had to seem traumatic to the sufferer to cause post-traumatic stress.

PTSD symptoms can include flashbacks, bad dreams, scary thoughts, and self-blame. People may avoid situations that trigger their stress response, which can include physical symptoms like sweating or a racing heartbeat.

Some people with eating disorders also have mood disorders such as depression or bipolar disorder.

Depression isn't just being sad or moping around. It's not just canceling plans because you're not in the mood. Depression affects your whole life. Its severity varies, but depression can cause irritability, decreased energy, feelings of guilt, feelings of unworthiness, a sad or anxious mood, appetite changes, changes in sleep patterns, and thoughts of death or suicide.[35]

Depression makes it hard to gain the motivation to recover from an eating disorder. In short, depression can make you hate yourself. Add that to the way malnutrition affects your brain, and recovery becomes even more difficult.

People with bipolar disorder suffer periods of depression interspersed with periods of elation, or mania.[36]

During manic periods, people with bipolar disorder may have a lot of energy or feel very jumpy, even irritable. They may believe they can do many things at once and take on lots of responsibilities. They can have trouble sleeping and do risky, dangerous things.

Depressive periods are the crash after all this energy. During a depressive episode, people with bipolar disorder can be sad and hopeless, have low energy, and feel worried about everything.

A 2011 study found that 14 percent of people with bipolar disorder also have an eating disorder.[37]

The good news is that therapists are trained to recognize these co-occurring conditions. They can help you understand how your eating disorder and any other disorders interact and what you can do to be the healthiest version of yourself you can be. Psychiatrists are also trained to understand how medication for various conditions affect your body and your brain.

Anxiety makes life seem a whole lot harder. But it is manageable.

There is help.

## EXERCISE: WHAT MAKES YOU ANXIOUS?

Take some time to think about instances when you feel anxious. What types of events or activities make you feel that way? How often does it happen? What do you think you can do to make those situations easier to deal with or get through?

# CHAPTER 7

## Tool Kit of Distress Tolerance Skills to Help with Anxiety

### Types of anxiety and techniques that can help

**DISTRESS TOLERANCE IS** one of the skills taught in most eating disorder recovery programs, and it can help you deal with anxiety.[38] Distress tolerance is the idea that by facing anxiety, you will learn—and you will teach your body—that anxiety can't get the best of you. That you can push through it. That you don't have to be overwhelmed by the signals your body is flooded with. If you simply wait out the anxiety and distract yourself, you'll prove there never was a threat to begin with.

Of course, many people do have problems that are legitimate threats. If you are faced with abuse or are afraid you're in danger, please talk to someone you trust. These situations *should* be sources of anxiety, and your feelings are prompting you to act and to reach out.

Distress tolerance isn't for legitimately dangerous situations. But what about anxieties about eating breakfast? Is eating breakfast a real threat? Does it make sense to fear eating breakfast so much that you turn to your eating disorder or start thinking terrible things about yourself?

What if you're anxious about going out with friends? If you panic about going out to dinner or to a birthday party, might it be because you don't want to eat in front of other people? Are you afraid you'll eat too much in front of them and lose control? If not, what do you think is causing your anxiety?

Even if you know you "shouldn't" be nervous in these situations, you may be. And that's okay. That's what distress tolerance will help you address.

Whatever the situation, you may be anxious and distressed. So how can you get rid of these feelings while not acting in ways that are harmful or that continue this cycle of anxiety?

You ride the wave. Researchers have set forth a theory that anxiety is like a wave: In every situation, your anxiety will start off low, rise and build to a crest, and then gradually fall once again.[39]

When you are nervous or afraid, it is important to remember that these feelings won't last forever, even if it feels as if they will. Your body cannot sustain this "fight, flight, or freeze" response forever, especially once it realizes that you aren't really going to die.

Things will calm down. You just have to distract yourself in the meantime, while your body surfs the wave. You want to get through the moment until the pain and fear pass. Instead of listening to your eating disorder, which may reduce your anxiety but will hurt you in the long run, you can use distress tolerance tools instead.

Instead of using an unhealthy coping mechanism like disordered eating or exercise, you can distract yourself. You can talk to a friend, or use the specific coping skills that I discuss in this chapter.

After a while of continuously using your new coping skills, the wave of anxiety won't crest as high. Riding the wave won't take as long. You'll have experience pushing back against your eating disorder urges so you won't be tempted to use them anymore.

That's how you reach recovery. That's how you calm the waves. But you'll never get there unless you first try to surf.

Distress tolerance tools are highly personal. What works for one person may not work for another. But if you can distract and soothe yourself until the pain passes, you will get through the moment without making things worse.

When you're anxious, it's hard to concentrate on anything else. You may be thinking about your body, eating or not eating, or what people think of you. You don't have the time or the brain space to worry about how to stop yourself from worrying because you're too busy already worrying!

That's why distress tolerance skills come with a bunch of handy-dandy acronyms and abbreviations so you can remember how to help yourself in the moment. Keep reminders of these tools nearby so that when you need help, you don't have to think too much. Try writing some of these techniques down on an index card and keeping it in your pocket, or if you have a phone, use it to take pictures of these pages. That way, when you need it, help will be right there.

You can pick and choose, too. You can try the skills that you know work best for you or you can try them all. You can also create your own ways of getting through your anxiety. It's important to remember that everything is individual and that you shouldn't feel constrained by the tips here.

## Distract

First of all, you can distract yourself. What kind of hobby or activity can you do that occupies a lot of your mind, and maybe even your body?

I used to play piano when I had urges to exercise. Moving my fingers across the keys helped pass the time until my anxiety wave crested and started to fall.

Lots of the people I met in treatment centers knit or crocheted. You may like to color or draw, watch TV or movies, listen to music, play games, talk to a friend, or use fidget toys (like fidget spinners, kinetic sand, spinner rings, or Rubik's Cubes).

The goal is to choose something that can occupy your attention for an extended period of time, so anything goes!

## Make a list of pros and cons

When trying to convince yourself not to use a harmful coping mechanism, weigh the pros (good things) and cons (bad things) about the situation. Ask yourself what would happen if you acted on what you're tempted to do. How would this bring yourself toward your goal of self-acceptance? What would happen if you sat with the anxiety instead?

A list of pros and cons will help you use logic instead of immediately turning to your harmful coping mechanism.

## IMPROVE the moment

When you feel anxiety, you know that riding this wave is going to be hard. It's going to be painful, and it will feel as if it's lasting forever. That's when you need to think about how to make the ride better. How can you IMPROVE the moment?

Here's our first fun acronym of the book!

## I—Imagery

You know how looking at art can relax you? Or how you might feel more at peace when you see a painting of a beach scene or those cute baby animals? Maybe you love pictures of old crumbling castles or lighthouses, or even those modern paintings with bright shapes and colors splashed across a canvas. When you're stressed, try to see one of those pictures in your mind. Paint a mental picture of whatever relaxes you. Escape into that image to forget about your anxiety.

## M—Meaning

If you can find meaning in your situation, it can be easier to bear. Obviously, having an eating disorder is awful. Obviously, being worried about your body all the time isn't what you want. You might be dealing with some other stressful things, too. But is there any positive outcome that could result from your being in this situation? Maybe you'll eventually find your calling helping others. Or you'll prove to yourself how strong you can be when you overcome this hurdle. Try to put yourself a few months or a year in the future, then look back at yourself now and lend some words of hope about how wonderful life will be someday.

## P—Prayer

If you're religious or believe in a higher power, you can pray for strength or guidance. Whatever prayer means to you—

and prayer can take the form of many things—you can call upon it to get you through a stressful situation.

## R—Relaxation

Relaxation is a way to ease the stress you feel when you're worried. It often involves focusing on your body to see what areas are tight and tense, often with deep breathing. Many people relax through yoga or some gentle stretching. You can even get a massage, if that's comfortable and affordable for you. Often if your body is calm, your mind will follow. I'll talk about relaxation in more depth in Chapter Ten.

## O—One Thing at a Time

The situation you're in right now may be awful. You may think that you will never feel better and that there's no point in trying.

This is where you need to remember that these single moments of rejecting bad coping mechanisms *do* matter. They build upon each other like links in a chain. And once those links add up, that chain will be strong enough to lock up your eating disorder and send it away for good.

This can only happen if you don't despair, though. Take each situation one at a time and moment by moment. Don't think about the past or the future or how you might feel tomorrow. Think about how you feel *now* and how to push through *that moment alone*.

## V—Vacation

I *wish* I could tell you to book a flight and go to Hawaii. It would be pretty amazing to do that whenever I was stressed. "Doctor's orders, everyone!" I'd exclaim, then I'd jump on a plane and spend a week at the beach.

Unfortunately, we all can't afford vacations. We *can* take vacations in our mind, though. Your imagination can take you anywhere you want to go.

Close your eyes for a minute and picture yourself somewhere relaxing. It might be a beach at sunset. It might be in courtside seats at a basketball game or riding a bike through a forest.

You can also take a literal vacation, even if you don't travel across the world. Take a walk to the park down the street. Call a friend and talk about your favorite TV show. Give your mind a vacation from what you're worried about.

## E—Encouragement

You might not be a cheerleader with pom-poms and the ability to do a cartwheel, but you can cheer for yourself. Give yourself a pep talk and remind yourself of all the challenges you've overcome before. You've been fighting to get better, and you're doing a great job. Tell yourself what a warrior you are and can be. This evidence can be your armor in this battle, too.

## Wise mind ACCEPTS

Deep down, you know that hurting yourself isn't the answer. You haven't done anything to deserve the agony of your disordered eating or overexercising, or all the hurtful things you might say to yourself. You know there's another way to live your life. You know what you have to do. You just don't really want to do it yet. Or you can't make yourself do it.

Please keep trying.

Researchers have coined the acronym ACCEPTS to describe activities to bring yourself back to this wise mind. Some of them may sound silly and simplistic, things a little kid might do for a project. But you're not aiming for sophistication here. All you want to do is ride the wave. Let these activities be your surfboard.

### A—Activity

Find an activity to distract yourself from the anxiety, one that gives you joy. It can be anything. Painting or coloring. Knitting. Reading comic books or playing a role-playing game. Writing a poem or watching cartoons. Anything! (Anything safe that won't trigger any of your eating disorder behaviors, that is.)

### C—Contributing

Do something to contribute to the world and focus your brain on someone else. Make a card for someone you care about.

Volunteer. Pack up a bunch of books you don't read and send them to a shelter or a classroom that needs them. Get involved in politics. March for a cause.

### C—Comparison

If you compare yourself with other people, usually you compare yourself with someone "better," right? The goal here is to do the opposite—instead of thinking about what you *don't* have, think about what you do have. Think about what you can be grateful for and what makes you different and valuable.

### E—Emotions

Try to push away your main emotion of fear or anxiety by using a positive, opposite emotion instead. If you're sad, listen to happy music. If you can't stop crying, read a silly book. Ask a friend to tell you a funny story or go see a light-hearted movie.

### P—Pushing Away

Simply tell yourself that you won't deal with these negative thoughts and urges right now. When you have a thought that gives you anxiety, picture a stop sign in your head. When you think bad things about yourself, tell yourself those thoughts aren't helpful.

### T—Thoughts

Distract yourself with other thoughts. Count as high as you can. Do a crossword puzzle. Think of all the prime numbers. Try to find every color of the rainbow in the room that you're in, or an item that begins with each letter of the alphabet. Occupy your mind so your harmful urges can't get through.

### S—Sensations

Engage in an experience where your body is distracted from what's going on around you. Smell a favorite scented body lotion or take a walk in a garden. I love the smell of bookstores, while others may love listening to loud music. You could take a hot shower. A cold shower, even—that's definitely shocking! You don't want to hurt yourself; rather, you want to engage your senses in a therapeutic manner.

## Self-soothe

In this category, therapists and professionals focus on using the five senses (taste, smell, sight, hearing, and touch) to distract yourself from your anxiety. The goal is to focus on your body in a gentle way, one that helps you realize that your body is enough as it is and that it deserves relaxation and joy.

When I was sick with my eating disorder, I created a self-soothing "tool kit." This was an actual box that contained items to help me relax and distract myself, along with reminders of additional coping skills I could use. When I got an urge to use my eating disorder, I would open up my little box and use a few of these self-soothing objects.

Here are a few options, although individual choices will vary tremendously:

## Taste
Tea or hot chocolate. A food associated with a positive memory. (Make sure not to choose a food that might trigger an eating disorder behavior.)

## Smell
Candles or scented lotion.

## Sight
Pictures of people you love. Note cards with positive sayings on them or cards from others expressing their belief in you. Photos of places you want to visit one day or things you want to do. Art supplies.

## Hearing
Your favorite songs. A white-noise app. The sounds of nature. Something funny on television.

## Touch
Play dough. A fidget toy or stress ball. Lotion. Nail polish.

At first, distress tolerance will be difficult. You might still feel anxious. Your brain might be loud, and your body may twitch. You could be tempted to do something that you know would be wrong. These urges will still be there, but over time and through practice, your brain will get quieter. You'll get better and better at riding the wave.

You may always have anxiety, and there's nothing wrong with that. Anxiety is part of the human condition. Now you have tools, though. Now you can take action.

## EXERCISE: MAKE YOUR OWN SELF-SOOTHING TOOL KIT

What items do you want to include in your self-soothing tool kit? Use this tool kit the next time you feel stressed or want to engage in eating disorder behaviors and bad coping mechanisms.

# CHAPTER 8

## Assertiveness, or "Use Your Voice"

### Trying to feel confident

**THERE ARE PEOPLE** out there who seem born with confidence. One of my friends is like this. From the time we were in elementary school, she never cared what people thought about her. When they insulted her haircut, she laughed. She ate dessert without a second thought. She broke up with guys and was broken up *with* and then moved on, still assured of her self-worth.

This friend was a foreign creature to me, as strange as a little green alien with two silver antennae. I didn't understand how she functioned. I didn't understand how her mind worked, just as she couldn't understand mine.

Why *didn't* I like myself?

Why *couldn't* I speak up for what I wanted?

And why wouldn't I let myself eat that dessert—it looked so delicious!

My friend and I needed a translator to get through to each other, and my work in recovery was that translator. It took me a long time to realize that it was possible for me to feel that same sense of belonging in my life, too.

When I had an eating disorder, I didn't like myself. I didn't think my voice was worth anything. You may feel the same way. You may feel as if you don't belong in your body, whether it's because of your size or your gender or something else. You may feel wrong. Faulty. Not "enough."

I didn't think I was "enough" to be an active participant in the world, to step forward and proclaim: "This is who I am!" I thought I'd be laughed at. I thought people would judge me and call me boring. A loser. Pretentious.

I was so afraid of judgment that I wouldn't let myself live. I wouldn't let myself take risks because I was afraid of rejection. I wouldn't reach out to make new friends because I was scared they wouldn't like me.

So instead of living, I turned inward. I thought about my body and weighed myself a lot. I got angry at my body for growing and developing the way bodies are *supposed* to when they go through puberty, when we're not trying to actively control them. I thought I didn't deserve to speak up, so I didn't.

## You might dislike yourself now, but you are special and deserve a voice

You may feel the exact same way I did. You may think that you're defective, that you need to hide behind a veil of disordered eating. Or you may hide behind a persona you've created, one that's harder to maintain every day.

You may not like who you are, but the combination of qualities that make you *you* are so important.

You *can't* be someone else, and you deserve to live and to be, just as you are. You deserve to ask for what you want. Part of embracing yourself will be to start using your voice, challenging your thoughts, tolerating anxiety, and putting yourself out there.

Once I realized that it was okay to be me, it became easier to take risks. I raised my hand in class more because if I gave the wrong answer, well, who cared? Yeah, I wouldn't be right, but in the end, was that so bad? The teacher would say no, and she'd call on another kid. Maybe that kid would be wrong, too.

## Learning to speak up to friends and family

Strangely, the hardest shift for me was learning how to be assertive with my friends and family, the people who were supposed to love me unconditionally but who often expected me to be soft-spoken and agreeable, to not speak up when I was angry. I realize that in this instance, I'm lucky. My family *does* love me, even if my parents criticize things I do occasionally. My friends *do* respect me, and the ones who didn't, I eventually removed from my life.

Some of you may not have such support systems around you. Your parents may work so much you never see them. Your classmates might make fun of you. Your best friends might be too far away to give you a hug when you need one.

Assertiveness is hard when you're met with rejection or with people who don't care.

It's still worth speaking up, though. You're still worth it. You deserve to ask for what you want and what you need.

**IMPORTANT NOTE:** If you're in a situation where you fear violence if you speak up for yourself, please speak to an adult you trust or seek professional help from a therapist or support group. Resources at the end of this book can help you connect with professionals.

## EXERCISE: WHAT ARE YOU AFRAID OF?

Make a list of things you have been afraid to ask for or speak up about. These could be actions you need people to take, comments you want people to stop making, or an issue that you feel strongly about.

Why haven't you been speaking your mind? What's the worst that could happen if you do?

# CHAPTER 9

## Cognitive Reframing, or How to Change Your Thoughts

### How cognitive behavioral therapy can help

**HAVE YOU EVER** told yourself that you aren't good enough: not smart enough, not thin enough, not nice enough, or not "enough" in some other way? I would estimate that on average teenagers think something negative about themselves every day. For some, this thinking could be constant.

Middle school and high school are times of transition. You're not in elementary school anymore, with parents watching over your shoulder every single minute, but you're not in college yet, living on your own.

You can make more decisions for yourself, but not all. You may get dropped off at the mall to hang out with your friends. You may date. You start to figure out who you are apart from your family.

Sometimes you might not like that someone very much.

I was a shy kid. At least, I always thought of myself as shy. I was okay answering questions in class. I was able to talk to strangers and even gave speeches in front of crowds at youth group gatherings. My heart pounded beforehand and my underarms always sweat while I did it (which was way more embarrassing than the speeches themselves), but I could speak in front of crowds and talk to strangers. It wasn't impossible.

So why did I consider myself shy? I had friends. I didn't hide away in my room all the time. I didn't *feel* confident, though. I was the type of kid who always thought people were judging me. When I walked into a room, I assumed everyone was analyzing my clothing choices, my hair, my body, and how ridiculous it was that my voice trembled when I asked a question.

At the time, I told myself that people didn't like me. I knew it. My mind thought of every possible insult that my peers could possibly throw, and some that no one but me would ever dream up. That's why I acted shy—not because I was scared of what *was happening*, but because I was afraid of what *could happen*. I knew that hurt could come at any second, and I was ready to protect myself.

I slouched and blushed because I wanted to disappear. I believed that if I disappeared, nobody could recognize my faults.

I didn't take risks or ask what I considered "silly ques-tions" because people might laugh at me. Call me names. Proclaim me a failure.

I thought I knew what everyone was going to say. And even when they didn't say it, I still heard those names in my head. I heard them loudly, even though *I* was the one insult-ing myself. *I* was the one causing myself all this misery and making myself pull away from the world.

Along with distress tolerance, another key skill I learned in treatment was cognitive reframing, a tool used in cogni-tive behavioral therapy. At its core, cognitive behavioral therapy is a treatment method that aims to lower your anxi-ety by changing your thoughts.

## Cognitive reframing

Say you have a painting you think is ugly. Maybe it has lots of colors you don't like, all swirled together. It might be in an ugly frame, one that makes it look even more depressing. You might stick this picture in the corner of a room because it makes you sad to look at it. The picture might make the whole room, even the whole house, look worse.

But what happens when you switch the frame to one that makes the colors look better and balances out the scene? The picture still might not be your favorite thing to look at, but at least you won't cringe. At least it won't ruin your day or your house.

This is what cognitive reframing is: taking a thought that makes you feel awful about yourself and changing or rewording that thought to make it neutral, or even positive. To make the ugly picture—and your worldview—a little less awful.

Entire courses are dedicated to cognitive behavioral therapy, so you're obviously not going to become an expert through this chapter. Mastering cognitive reframing takes practice and time because it can be hard to realize that some of the messages you've been sending to yourself for your whole life are, in fact, a lie. They make so much sense in your head, after all!

## How thoughts, feelings, and emotions are connected

Deep down, a part of your brain knows that the bad things you think about your weight and yourself may not be true. It's the same part that led you to pick up this book. It's the same part that believes in a life without disordered eating.

Your thoughts *are* important. But they are not always correct, such as when you think bad things about yourself. Somewhere inside of you, you know this. You know you are worthy. You know you are enough.

Cognitive behavioral therapy is based upon the idea that your thoughts, your feelings, and your actions are all inter-related. When you have a thought, a specific feeling is naturally going to follow. If you think something bad about yourself, you will probably feel bad. You may sink into a bad mood. You may isolate yourself from others. If you have a positive thought, however, you'll probably feel good. You may smile. Maybe you'll do a good deed. You may take a risk that pays off.

Cognitive behavioral therapy is about changing all three of these things: your thoughts, your feelings, and your behavior. If you change your thinking so that you feel good, you're more likely to do something that's good for you.

That's the positive side of the cycle. But what happens when your negative thought leads to a negative feeling? You might think something bad, feel bad, and then do something that hurts yourself, like engaging in disordered eating, purging, or too much exercise. You might think, *Why not? Everyone hates me already.*

That's the negative side of the cycle, which keeps repeating itself over and over again. As you engage in disordered eating and other harmful coping mechanisms, you'll start to feel bad. And so it goes, again and again, until recovery seems further and further away.

The cycle always completes itself. Thoughts lead to feelings, which lead to behaviors. Behaviors twist back around to more thoughts and feelings. If you don't take a step back and recognize how endless this cycle can be, you'll get stuck in it. You'll waste your entire life feeling not good enough or punishing yourself for something you didn't do wrong at all.

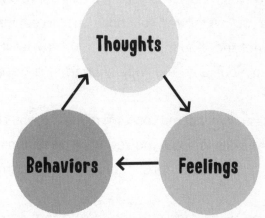

So how do you reframe your thoughts? And what if you don't believe yourself when you do it?

You might *not* believe yourself at first. That's the hard part. You may try to reframe a thought and *still* feel awful because you don't believe this reimagined truth in the slightest.

That doesn't mean that cognitive reframing will never work. You need practice and repetition to believe anything, especially statements that go against what you've seen as the truth for months or even years.

You can change your thoughts. You can change your behavior. Just take it one situation at a time.

For example, you might think, *I don't like what my body looks like. That means I'm a failure.*

At first, you might not realize there's anything to reframe here. If you think this, you may believe it's true. After all, why would your head lie to you? You may tell yourself that of course you're a failure if your body isn't "acceptable." You may accept the thought instantly. You may let it affect the rest of your day. You may engage in a destructive behavior.

But if you know about cognitive reframing, you can use these new skills instead; you can work on reframing that harmful thought so it doesn't affect your mood or your actions.

For you, your *reaction*—the feeling that you are a failure—is a distortion. It is based on the skewed logic of your eating disorder rather than the truth. When you have an eating disorder, many of your *feelings*, especially the anxious ones, are distorted and twisted by other people's comments, by your own feelings about your body, or by the messages we get from the media and society that however you look is "unacceptable."

## Learning to accept others' opinions—even when they're negative

What would you think if your frenemy walked up to you and said, "Nice outfit"? Would you believe them? Or would your mind automatically jump to the conclusion that they're being sarcastic, that your outfit is hideous and that no one will ever like you?

I jumped to conclusions like that a lot. (And then I felt bad about myself all day, skipped dinner, and ran to punish myself.)

**Thought:**
"They're being sarcastic and think I look hideous."

**Feeling:**
Ashamed and self-conscious

**Behavior:**
Engaged in eating disordered actions

But what would happen if you chose to believe that person instead? If you said, "Thanks, I like this outfit, too." You'd probably feel happy. You might go on with your day that much more confident. You'd probably feel great and would treat your body well.

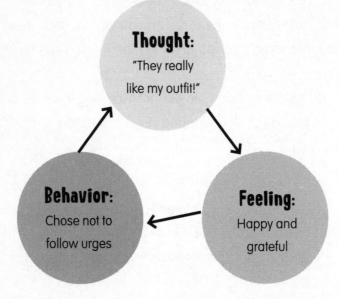

You deserve to treat your body well. Because even if some random person does insult you some day, that's just their opinion. Here is another tactic you can take: You can accept that someone *is* actually insulting or making fun of you.

But instead of letting that judgment run—and ruin—your life, what about focusing on this thought instead: *That's just their opinion.*

Those are four powerful words:

*That's just their opinion.*

Realizing the truth and meaning behind this sentence changed my life:

*I don't have to care about what other people think.*

Repeat it after me. (Or if it would be way too embarrassing to speak out loud right now, think it. You can say it later. You can say it all you want, for the rest of your life.)

*I don't have to care about what other people think. I can't make everyone happy. This is just their opinion, and it's no better than mine.*

Imagine how your life would change if you believed this. If you lived this.

You wouldn't have to buy certain brands of clothes because they're in fashion even though they're super uncomfortable.

You could act silly in the lunchroom without worrying what "people" will think about you.

You wouldn't have to join clubs or do sports you dislike simply to gain your peers' or your parents' approval.

You could have crushes on the people you like.

You could stop manipulating your body and let it be what it is meant to be.

You are your own person. Let other people judge themselves. *You* can judge you.

Or not.

Because that's what we're all learning here. What I'm still learning. I don't *have* to judge myself. It's not a requirement for being human.

When I start thinking that I'm a failure, when I look in the mirror and don't like how I look, I don't *have* to feel awful about it. I don't have to do anything to fix myself.

I am not my thoughts. No one is forcing me to obey them. I can stop, examine my thoughts, and make a decision on my own, based on what I want my future to look like. I may have to reframe my thoughts, but I never have to reframe myself.

I am enough. So are you.

## EXERCISE: WATCHING YOUR THOUGHT CYCLE

Make a list of all the negative thoughts and judgments you may have in a half hour. See if you can trace these thoughts through the thought-feeling-behavior cycle. Try to think of a different thought you can substitute next time.

For example, if you look in the mirror and see a pimple on your nose, you might automatically think that you look ugly. But what if you substituted this thought instead: *Most people have to deal with pimples, so I'm not alone and this isn't a big deal.*

Instead of feeling bad about yourself and hiding from the world, you might realize that what you're going through is totally normal. You'll interact with people and smile. You'll have a good day instead of one shadowed by pimply clouds.

Maybe a classmate makes fun of you when you drop your tray in the cafeteria, which makes you automatically think that you're a loser and will never fit in.

But what if you instead told yourself that everyone makes mistakes? What if you laughed at yourself and maybe even took a bow? Instead of punishing yourself because one person might dislike you, you can tell yourself that everyone doesn't *have* to approve of what you do. And that anyone who dislikes you because you dropped a tray (or for any other reason!) isn't worth your time anyway.

What kind of examples can you think of in your life?

## EXERCISE: CHANGING NEGATIVE THOUGHTS

If you can, try to change a negative thought the moment it occurs. What happens? Is it hard? After you changed the thought, did you end up doing something different from what you usually do after a negative thought?

# CHAPTER 10
## Why Relaxation Is Important

### Relaxation can be hard

**CLOSE YOUR EYES** and take a deep breath. In and out. Now count to ten, slowly, and try not to let your mind wander. One, two, three . . .

Did you find that difficult? If so, you're not alone. Even though I know how important relaxation is, I'm awful at it. Forced relaxation, that is. I've tried meditation. I've tried yoga. I've tried the whole mindfulness thing where you stare at a raisin for a full minute to examine how it looks, then put it in your mouth to really experience the taste. At the time, this exercise felt extremely odd to me. It's a raisin. Can I just pop it in my mouth and get on with eating the next raisin?

As you can see, I have always struggled to relax. I still do today, but have found some techniques that work for me.

# How I struggled with relaxation

When I was in treatment for my eating disorder, I did not know how to sit still. Part of this was because of my intense desire to burn off the calories I was ingesting, but most of this antsiness came from my anxiety. My treatment team (the set of doctors, nutritionists, and counselors at my treatment center) kept telling me to trust them—that everything would be okay when I followed the course of treatment—but I couldn't let myself believe them quite yet.

I didn't understand this new world I had stepped into, a world where what I thought was true was all wrong. Where I had to trust other people and my own body above all else.

I was afraid. I was scared. I wanted to run. At the very least, I wanted to bounce my leg up and down all day long. How was I supposed to do a silly relaxation exercise before a meal if my heart was pounding out of my chest? How would stretching and yoga make me feel better when I was used to running?

How? How? How?

Here's what I should have been saying: Yes. Yes. Yes.

Because my treatment team was right. (They usually were. I hated how that always happened. It's like how I got older and realized that my parents actually know what they're talking about.) I needed to relax and let go. Trust that someone would catch me when I fell. Trust that my *body* would catch me when I fell.

## Relaxation is important for recovery

You know those free-fall trust exercises? The ones where you cross your arms over your chest, then fall backward without buckling or trying to save yourself? Where someone else has to catch you, someone you might not know very well, someone you might not even like very much?

That's what recovery is like. Standing tall and trusting. Leaning and not resisting. Trusting what you think shouldn't be trusted at all.

Relaxing into yourself and welcoming who you are with open arms. And if not with open arms, then at least by not pushing yourself and your feelings away.

Relaxing into yourself also means actually *relaxing*: doing something without distracting yourself with obsessions or the constant need to do more, move more, or achieve more.

## Learning to be still

Relaxation is still hard for me. Even now, when I *don't* hate my body, when I *don't* think about weight loss every hour of every day, I still like to *do*. I like to get things done. I like to read as much as I can and work on my next book idea. I like to scroll through the latest news and see what my friends are talking about online. I like to be connected.

I'm still learning that it's okay to be disconnected. That simply being with myself is okay. That I don't have to multi-task while I'm watching TV. (This is still a constant source of discussion between me and my husband, who gets irritated when I miss out on a piece of dialogue because I'm looking at my phone.) I don't have to scroll through social media or do a crossword puzzle at the same time as I watch a movie. There's no one keeping a scorecard of how much I get done in a certain day.

## What are some ways you can relax?

You may be someone who always focuses on goals or achievement, but for me, doing something that makes me happy or relaxed is an achievement by itself.

People need relaxation. And relaxation can help you deal with your disordered eating. Here are a few ways to try to relax.

### Yoga

Yoga forces you to slow down and be aware, to notice how the different parts of your body interact with each other and to see how, no matter what your size, you can move and flow and be strong. Many studies have found that doing yoga helps individuals grow to accept, if not love, their bodies. A twelve-week study of adolescent girls with eating disorders in 2016 showed that doing yoga led to a decrease in depression, anxiety, and concerns about weight and shape.[40]

Any size body can do yoga, too. In fact, a growing segment of the yoga community embraces and celebrates larger sizes. Many disabled people can do yoga; yoga positions can be modified according to a person's ability. If you're taking a yoga class, yoga teachers can help you come up with poses that are comfortable for you—they're trained in this.

## Sleep

Sleep is pretty great, too. This may sound silly and oh so obvious, but every body needs sleep. Regular sleep keeps your brain working, heals your body and your heart, and helps with decision-making and regulating emotions. But many kids don't get the sleep they need. The National Sleep Foundation states that only 15 percent of teens reported sleeping for eight and a half hours on school nights. But teens need eight to ten hours of sleep per night to function at peak effectiveness and alertness.[41]

And, honestly, why wouldn't you want to be at peak alertness? Peak alertness is when you can experience life the most. When you're able to concentrate in school the best, remember what you studied for tests, and play hard during sports practice. Sleep is good. I like sleep.

Sleep is just as important as food and water. Sleep allows your muscles to heal from the activities of the day. It lets your brain consolidate memories and lets your body recharge.

The National Sleep Foundation states that when people drive while sleep-deprived, it's just as dangerous as driving drunk. The human body is *that* incapacitated by being overtired.[42]

Sleep is also an important part of recovery.

In her recovery, biology student Michelle has made self-care a priority despite her busy schedule. "I know that anxiety about food is heightened when I'm running on little sleep; I recognize that I tend toward restrictive behaviors during these periods," she said. "Recovery is maintaining a firm commitment to a stable sleep schedule, even when it's difficult because of social obligations or classes."[43]

Imagine what exhaustion does to your decision-making skills. You *need* to be alert when you're navigating a world that's trying to convince you that you're not enough the way you are.

Listening to your body applies to rest just as much as food. You are allowed to take a time-out from the world. Rest and relax so you can wake up as fully able to be kind to yourself as possible.

## Mindfulness exercises

When you are aware of something, you are mindful of it.[44] You are present in the moment, feeling your feelings and accepting what is going on. Specific exercises can help you develop this quality of "mindfulness," which is often way harder than it sounds.

In theory, it should be easy to focus on one thing. But our minds wander a lot! We hear a noise and wonder what it is. We feel an itch on our elbow. Then we think about that thing our friend told us at lunch. We wonder what's for dinner. We wonder if we should eat something else for dinner instead.

Then, without even realizing it, we're not in the moment at all!

This does not mean that you've failed at mindfulness, though. Minds wander. Minds think. It is what they do. Mindfulness training teaches you to accept that your mind *will* wander and how to gently bring it back to what you are trying to focus on.

The raisin exercise I mentioned earlier is commonly used to help people think of food beyond its connection to weight and body. Food has a smell, taste, and texture. It can bring joy.

Deep breathing is another mindfulness exercise to help people center themselves. When your thoughts are spinning and you can't stop obsessing, trying to focus on one thing—your breathing—can help push those worries aside.

Being mindful can help with body acceptance because being mindful *is* being accepting: One can't exist without the other. Here's an exercise that will help you understand:

## EXERCISE: CONNECT WITH YOUR BODY

Lie with your eyes closed and breathe in deeply. Listen to the noises around you. Feel your arms wherever they're resting. How do they feel? Feel your heels against the floor and your hair against your face. Which parts of your body feel tense? If your mind wanders, bring it back to the present moment, to your body.

During mindfulness exercises, you are not trying to determine the size or shape of your body or whether it's changed. Instead, these exercises are meant to help you notice your place in the world and to show you that you do not take up "too little" space or "too much" space. You are simply here, touching the earth and breathing in and out.

You are a person.

You are here.

You do not have to think about this morning or tomorrow.

You do not have to think about five minutes from now.

You are only in this single moment.

You don't have to do anything or achieve anything.

You are here and you are present.

There is no competition and no pressure.

There is just you.

Mindfulness can sound like a bunch of airy-fairy non-sense to some people. It sounded like that to me at first. But now I realize that it really *can* be helpful to take a break, to give myself permission—or have someone *else* give me permission—to step back and breathe.

Just breathe.

**NOTE**: If you cannot find or afford a meditation, mindfulness, or yoga class near you (or if you don't yet feel comfortable relaxing in front of a group), there are many apps that your parents can help you download for free or a low cost. YouTube has a number of meditation and relaxation videos you can follow along with. Many community centers often offer yoga and meditation classes at reduced rates, as do public libraries, which usually go one step further and offer classes for free!

## EXERCISE: A PEACEFUL MINUTE

Stay still and quiet for a minute. You can sit, stand, or lie down for this, but you do have to be still. Breathing is all you have to do. Set a timer, then breathe in and out. Try to inhale for five seconds, then exhale for five seconds. Breathe in through your nose and out through your mouth, only focusing on those breaths. But breathe deeply. Let the air fill your whole lungs. This will mean that your stomach needs to expand out, but that's okay. Every time you think about something that's not your breathing, bring your mind back to those ins and outs.

How many times did your mind wander? Did this exercise make you uncomfortable or anxious? Why?

## EXERCISE: OBJECT STUDY

Pick an object near you. The object doesn't have to be a raisin, but it should be something non-human. Focus on that object and describe it to yourself. What does it look like? Is it curved? Sharp? Smooth? What color is it? What shade? What purpose does it have? How does it look in comparison with other objects around it? If you can touch it, how does it feel? Smell? Is it something you can hear or taste?

When you're done, think about this object and its place in the world. Do you have a place, too—you with all your unique characteristics?

# CHAPTER 11

## Who's This "Ed" Guy? (One Way to Think About Your Eating Disorder)

### It helps some people to think of their eating disorder as a person

**FOR MANY PEOPLE** dealing with eating disorders, "Ed" is the name they give their disease. It's a way to separate themselves from the voice in their head telling them to engage in disordered eating or exercise.

Ed is the whisper in their ear telling them they're not good enough, the scream yelling at them to do more and *be* more.

Author and eating disorder recovery advocate Jenni Schaefer talked about this imaginary Ed in her 2003 book *Life Without Ed*, which she expanded upon in its sequel, *Goodbye Ed, Hello Me*.

When I say "imaginary," I don't mean that Ed isn't real. I don't mean that he *is* real, either. (Or she, or whatever gender your Ed is. I use *he/him* pronouns here because that's how Jenni Schaefer refers to Ed.)

Ed is both real *and* "all in your head." That's because he's the voice *in* your head telling you to do things that you know will hurt your body. He's part of you, but he isn't the "true" you at all.

It sounds weird, right? The whole Ed thing sounds like something you'd never want to admit to another person, lest they think you're imagining things. You don't want to admit that you hear voices in your head.

I did, though. I still do, sometimes. They're soft as a whisper now, but every so often, when I'm stressed or down on myself, I hear them:

*You're not a good person.*

*You'll never get all your work done.*

*You'll feel better if you go for a run.*

Before, when I was really sick with my eating disorder, Ed's voice was louder. The whispers were more like yells. They were booming and overwhelming, like the sound of fire engines' sirens at a Fourth of July parade. Even if I put my hands over my ears, they were still there. Their echoes lasted, too, swirling around in my head until I had no choice but to obey, by engaging in disordered eating and exercise.

I was flooded with negative thoughts about myself. All those messages came from Ed. Ed is mean. Ed didn't like me. Ed didn't want me to recover. He didn't want me to like myself because then he'd have nothing to do. He'd be out of a job. And that would make Ed sad.

That's good, though. In recovery, your *job* is to make Ed sad.

Schaefer likes to look at Ed as a separate person, one you need to fight back against. One you don't need to listen to. You can think of Ed as a mean significant other or partner. Or a "friend" who doesn't have your best interests at heart. Ed can be like a grandparent who always pinches your cheeks and criticizes every little thing you do because your behavior isn't "proper enough."

Whoever Ed is, he's someone you don't want in your life. He's someone who makes you feel bad about yourself and who doesn't care about you. Why would you want to listen to someone who constantly criticizes and emotionally abuses you? Would you stand that kind of behavior from a friend?

I definitely wouldn't. I'd talk to my friend about how much of a jerk she was being. Then if she didn't change, she wouldn't have a place in my life.

That's why it can be helpful to distinguish Ed from ourselves. When you separate out the messages an eating disorder sends you—the messages you hear so often that they start to seem like reality—it can become easier to fight back against them.

It can be easier to yell at Ed to shut up.

# How to talk to Ed

You can speak to Ed out loud. If you're alone in your room and it's helpful to literally tell Ed that he is wrong, go for it. Don't be embarrassed. Yell! Anything that helps you take your power back and show your eating disorder that you are the one in charge of your life. Even if you're not alone, you can still talk out loud.

You can also argue with Ed in your head. If your eating disorder tells you that you shouldn't keep eating according to your meal plan, you can retort back that your body needs fuel to live your life.

If your eating disorder tells you that life is too over-whelming and disordered eating will make you feel better, you can say that you have other ways to calm your emotions now.

If your eating disorder tells you that you can't hang out with your friends because you need to exercise, you can tell him that making memories is more important than a workout.

You can tell Ed that you're in charge.

Then you can imagine Ed disappearing in a puff of smoke.

In reality, it's not that easy. You won't always have a response for everything Ed throws at you because that guy is tricky. He's sneaky. He's aware of every single one of your weaknesses. If you're a creaky old house, Ed is the gust of wind that knows every single crack it can sneak into to make your life colder and colder.

## Finding your voice amid the clamor of Ed's

If you keep separating out Ed's voice from your own, you'll get to know what he sounds like and what his common tricks are.

And if you keep challenging that little voice inside your head, you'll start to realize that Ed's words aren't orders you have to follow. They're actually really mean commentaries on your life that *you can choose to ignore*. That's right! You can disobey Ed. And the more you do, the easier it becomes. You'll be able to predict the types of things Ed might say and identify how those messages make you feel.

You'll be able to talk back and do the opposite action.

Maybe at first you'll only be able to identify Ed's messages. That's okay. It's still a step in the right direction.

Maybe at first you'll be able to talk back to the voice, but you won't be able to disobey it. That's okay, too.

Maybe you'll start doing things that go against what Ed wants, but then you'll feel guilty. You'll feel like you did something wrong. You'll feel full or you'll binge or you'll compare yourself with someone else and despair. You'll slip and go back to behaviors that you know aren't the healthiest.

That's okay. You can slip. Just as you can always pick yourself up again.

Because here's the important part—once you realize that Ed's messages are completely separate and different from the healthy actions you know will lead you toward a happy life, you can unlearn Ed's beliefs and start to follow healthier ones. You'll hear that voice in your head and know that it's Ed. And your Ed doesn't have to be human, either: For you, Ed may be a seven-fingered, purple-nosed alien from the planet Norblak.

You can picture Ed however you want. You just need to push Ed out of your life.

However you picture Ed, he doesn't have to be with you forever. If you don't want a purple-nosed alien in your life, you don't have to have one. You'd break up with someone who always calls you names, so why don't you do the same thing with Ed?

Remember, Ed may appear anywhere at any time: when you're eating with friends, when a caregiver criticizes your food choices, when your friends are busy on a Friday night and you're alone in your room, when you step onto the scale and the number isn't what you expected, or wanted, to see.

When you don't feel "enough."

That's not *your* voice yelling in your head. That's your eating disorder's. That's Ed's.

Talk back to him.

Yell at him.

Tell him that you won't listen. Then *don't* listen.

Over time, the voice will get quieter and quieter.

It may disappear entirely. It may not. But even if it doesn't, now that you know how it sounds, you never have to listen to that whisper again.

## What if the idea of Ed doesn't work for you?

Sometimes the idea of Ed worked for me. Sometimes it was helpful to separate myself from my eating disorder and the mean messages it was giving me. If Ed was a different person, I could ignore him. I could banish him. Then I'd be *me* again. And if I was just me, I could be healthy. I wouldn't be sick or anxious or have people worried about me anymore.

That never happened, though, even when I made a conscious effort to identify the eating disorder voice. When I made a list of things Ed said and combated those insults and orders with my healthy voice, the anxieties and fears were still there. When I did the direct opposite of what Ed wanted, I was still afraid.

I didn't know why. Was I doing things wrong? Was my Ed different from everyone else's? Was I never going to recover?

I thought I was broken.

I wasn't broken; I was recovering. One super annoying thing is that recovery doesn't happen instantaneously. Even once you make the decision that you want to get better, that life with an eating disorder is unbearable, and that you'd rather do something scary than live one more day hungry and weight-obsessed—even then, there are ups and downs and steps backward.

Recovery is a process. It can take months. It can take years. All in all, the "official" length of my eating disorder and recovery—from when I started to diet and worry about my weight to when I finally let go of the teeny-tiny "I don't really think this is a problem because people without eating disorders do stuff like this, too" behaviors that kept me stuck in "almost recovery"—was twelve years.

Twelve years! That's a long time. Of course, every second of those twelve years wasn't misery. My sickness during that time took various levels of intensity, from "in the hospital" sick to "a healthy weight but still not letting myself have exactly what I want to eat" sick to "still wanting to be perfect" sick.

Recovery *isn't* perfect. Recovery isn't a straight line. As I mentioned before, recovery is ups and downs and squiggles and U-turns and doubling back. It's making progress, then getting scared and retreating back to your shell of safety.

Your eating disorder feels safe to you. It may not be fun, and it may make you miserable and sad, but it still feels safe. You know what to expect when you're dieting and purging and planning what to do each day. You're good at being body-obsessed. Your body can be controlled.

Recovery can't be controlled. Yes, there are meal plans and appointments and schedules you have to follow. There's accountability. And for many of you, there's nagging. There are people watching you to make sure you do the right thing.

But you can't predict how you're going to feel every day in recovery. Some mornings you might wake up ready to take on the world and show your eating disorder who's boss. Some mornings you might wake up, look in the mirror, and immediately feel gross. You may immediately want to do "something" to fix yourself, even though there is probably nothing to fix at all.

So if Ed doesn't work for you, try not to feel bad about it. Ed is a helpful concept for a lot of people. But if you don't like to think of Ed as a separate entity outside of yourself, that's okay, too. This idea doesn't work for everyone. Some people like to think of this Ed voice as *part* of them, something that's linked to who they are and their unique personality.

### EXERCISE: THE THINGS ED SAYS

Make a list of all the things Ed says to you in a day. If you feel able to, respond to them in a way that you consider healthy. Which of Ed's messages could you ignore in the future? What would be some kinder things to say to yourself instead?

# CHAPTER 12
## Admitting Struggles and Being Vulnerable

### It's okay to realize that you need help

**IT'S HARD TO** admit that you're wrong.

It's hard to admit that you don't know what you're doing.

It's hard to admit that you're flawed and not "as good as" everyone else.

As humans, we try to avoid this state of "wrongness" from the time we're little kids. We draw on the wall with marker and emphatically declare that it wasn't us, even when ink is smudged all over our hands. We vehemently shake our heads after throwing a ball in the house and accidentally knocking over a parent's favorite vase. Of course we didn't do that; it was just the wind. Oh, the window wasn't open? Well, then it was a ghost. Totally a ghost.

We deny because we don't want to get in trouble, but we also deny because we don't want to disappoint people.

We don't admit when we're having trouble.

We don't admit when we need help.

## My eating disorder happened gradually, and I didn't think I could ask for help

When I was first getting sick with an eating disorder, it didn't happen all at once. I didn't decide that I wanted to lose weight and then all of a sudden start starving myself. It was more gradual than that. I ate a little less and exercised a little more. I got positive feedback for these actions and realized that I felt more in control of my life.

So I kept going. Soon, though, I realized that the things I was doing *weren't* actually making me feel better. They weren't making my life better, but now they were compulsions—they had taken control of me.

After a while, after I became really sick, I *couldn't* make myself eat more. I *couldn't* make myself exercise less. Even when I realized how miserable I was and decided I wanted to get better—I couldn't stop myself. It was as if my brain and my heart lived in two different dimensions; they spoke two different languages and couldn't communicate, no matter how hard I tried to make myself act in a healthy way.

*I don't want to be sick anymore,* I told my body and my mind. *Stop!*

I couldn't stop. If I tried to eat more, I felt a tightening in my chest. My body seized up and panic overtook me. If I stopped just one minute short of my regular exercise session, my body expanded. I had gained one hundred pounds in that one minute, I was sure of it, even though that statement made no logical sense whatsoever.

I knew that I needed help to get better, but I couldn't bring myself to ask for that help. If I asked for help, it would mean that I wasn't the perfect student/perfect daughter/perfect girl I was supposed to be—the one everyone always thought I was. I'd destroy that illusion. And without that illusion, who would I be? I'd be the girl with a mental illness, the one who couldn't do something as simple as eat on her own.

I couldn't let anyone think that. I couldn't be "that girl."

So instead I was the *other* girl. The girl who struggled alone. The girl who canceled plans and lost her friends because she didn't want them around. If they were around, they would see that something was wrong. They'd ask questions.

I became the girl who suffered in silence and didn't let anyone inside. The one who missed out on parties and dates and late-night chats because she was afraid of being found out. I didn't let anyone in, so nobody came in. I was alone.

I eventually got found out, of course, when my dad

busted me on the exercise bike in the middle of a work day. Before that, my parents had probably picked up on some clues. They saw me eating smaller meals and losing weight. They questioned if I was *really* going to eat breakfast on the way to school or if I'd *really* gone out for dinner with friends. They had all the puzzle pieces, but they hadn't put them together. They didn't see the whole picture yet, but that day, my dad stumbled upon the last piece, and my parents saw what had been there all along: a very sick daughter.

That's when I went into treatment for the first time. That's when therapists and counselors and nutritionists encouraged me to tell them what was going on, to let them know what I was afraid of. They told me to journal about my fears and struggles and speak up in groups about how hard this whole "recovery thing" was.

I didn't do any of those things. Even though I had been pulled out of school, even though I was staying overnight in the hospital, even though I was obviously sick, I was still afraid of telling people that I was having trouble.

*Of course* I was having trouble. Duh! (Remember, even if you don't go into treatment, you can still be having trouble. There is no achievement you need to reach before you can ask for help.)

I didn't want to *say* I was sick, though. Saying the words and admitting that I had a problem would make it real. And I didn't want to make it real, even as I was discharged from the hospital and then almost immediately sent back again because I had relapsed.

I didn't have a problem. (So I ate my new meal plan and smiled the whole time.)

I didn't have a problem. (So I told people how easy things were and how much better I was getting.)

I didn't have a problem. (So I kept relapsing.)

In my mind, I wasn't smiling. Eating food and stopping all exercise wasn't easy. It hurt my body, and it made my mind anxious. I didn't want to do it in treatment, and I didn't want to do it when I left.

I didn't tell anyone this, though. I didn't want them to know that I wasn't the perfect girl or the perfect patient. And because I didn't tell anyone, no one could help me.

That's why I relapsed. Not because recovery is hard. (It *is* hard, yes, but it's *impossible* without being open about things.) I relapsed because I wasn't honest. I wasn't vulnerable. The only way to make recovery easier—to make recovery possible—is to talk about it, to discuss the hard parts and to get help wading through them.

I was in and out of treatment a lot before I was honest with myself. It took even longer before I was honest with my doctors and my nutritionist. I was ashamed to be sick. Ashamed to be broken. Afraid to be vulnerable. So I kept all my struggles inside. And they grew and grew and grew.

I hid things like this a lot. I still hide my true feelings

sometimes, in areas that don't have anything to do with food. It's hard to admit that I'm not keeping up with everything. That some days I get randomly sad. That every single laundry basket in the house is overflowing. That I canceled dinner with my friend last week because I was so stressed out about other things.

I do get sad, though. I do make mistakes.

I'm human.

## You might feel scared and alone, but it's okay to reach out

It might be the same for you.

If you've recently changed schools, is it hard to admit that the new building is way too big and kind of scary?

If you can't understand something that's going on in class but every single other person seems to know instinctively what's going on, do you hesitate before raising your hand and asking for an explanation? Do you ask for an explanation at all?

If you didn't make the softball team and your parents were expecting you to, are you afraid to tell them?

If you get dumped, is it hard to tell your friends?

If you get teased every day at school, do you tell a parent? Or do you let your family keep thinking that you're the most popular kid in school?

Why?

Why is it so hard to admit that we have problems? Why is it so hard to admit that we struggle and fall and fail and hurt?

Everyone hurts. Everyone falls. It might not seem that way, but I promise that every single kid in your grade has some sort of problem. Their problems might not be as bad as yours, and they might not be having them right now, but every person still has problems. No one's life is perfect.

Let me repeat that: No one's life is perfect.

*You* aren't expected to be perfect, either. In fact, when you pretend to be perfect, as I did, when I wouldn't tell anyone that I was sick or when I told everyone that recovery was all sparkles and unicorns—well, then you just end up hurting even worse.

I often wonder what would have happened if I had told people that I was struggling with food and recovery. That I was worried about my body and couldn't make myself eat more, even though my stomach was angrily demanding to be fed. Maybe I wouldn't have been sick for as long as I was.

Maybe. Maybe not.

I don't know. What I do know is that in my life now I try my best to be honest. I don't always succeed. I might have a bad day and tell my mother that things are fine when she asks because I really don't want to get into the details. I might tell my husband that I'm okay, even though I woke up feeling anxious for some reason.

These are little things, though, and I do them so that my loved ones won't worry. But if these little things ever become *big* things, I know it's time for me to open my mouth and tell the truth.

I am vulnerable. I hurt. I make mistakes, lots of them.

I am still worthy, though. Even when I was sick, I was worthy. People didn't think less of me because I asked them for help. They thought more of me, actually. They respected me for speaking up. They *wanted* to help.

## What if you don't know where to turn for help?

If you don't think that you have anyone in your life right now who can help you, please keep looking. So many communities are out there waiting with open arms to let you in. There are support groups for queer kids and teens. There are groups specifically for boys with eating disorders and groups for specific ages. There are teachers and adults and peers who are willing to listen and help if your home life feels unstable.

You can and will find people who can help, whether it's helping you recover and get your disordered eating under control or simply listening to you cry about losing a relationship or failing a test. If they matter—if they're worth it—people will listen.

They will help.

## EXERCISE: THE THINGS YOU'RE AFRAID TO SAY

What are some things you're afraid to tell people about yourself? If it's hard to write these things down, list them in your head. For each item, write what you think would happen if you told people about it. What would they say? Do? How would you feel? How would telling someone help?

If you can, choose one thing you're struggling with and choose someone to confide in. Plan out what you're going to say. You can even preface the talk with how you're nervous. What happens?

# PART THREE

Society, Role Models,
Family, and Media

# CHAPTER 13

## BMI and Why It's Nonsense

### Why BMI exists

**ONE FLAWED MEASUREMENT** that doctors—and society—obsess over is BMI.

Body mass index is a calculation that a lot of people think is important, but that doesn't actually show much about a person's overall health. It's just a number determined by your weight and height. The theory is that by looking at this ratio, doctors will be able to screen more easily for people at risk for potential health problems.

So depending on this number, people are sorted into categories: "underweight," "normal weight," "overweight," or "obese." If someone is "obese" or "overweight," that person may be perceived as being less healthy than someone who's a "normal" weight. If people are a "normal" weight, they may be seen as being more healthy.

But the truth is that BMI is arbitrary. The classifications are arbitrary. So arbitrary, in fact, that in 1998 the BMI scale was changed, lowering the cutoffs for each category and instantly reclassifying millions of once "normal weight" people as "overweight" or "obese."[45]

## "obese" is a made-up label

How would our world and the way we feel about ourselves change if we didn't have to lose weight? If "obese" people weren't *expected* to lose weight?

People who are considered "obese" can be healthy. They can have normal blood pressure and a healthy heart. People who are considered "obese" can also be ill.

Thin people can get sick, too, just as thin people can be healthy.

This is why it's important for medical professionals to focus on the individual. What is that *one* specific patient experiencing? What are the individual's symptoms, regardless of body size? How can those symptoms be treated?

Our society needs to stop demonizing certain body types. Healthy or not, in shape or not, everyone deserves care and respect.

In this book I only use "obese" (in quotation marks) as an official medical term. Many activists prefer *fat* as the descriptive word, so I choose to use it instead. "Fat" is not a